Advance Praise for

Make Legal U-Turn When Necessary

"This book is unlike any other I've read before. In her autobiographical adventure from Wisconsin to California and back again, Ally proves that with the bond of family, a faith in God and sheer grit and determination, a woman can do anything she sets her mind to. With playful wording and sublime imagery throughout the entire story, she helps me to regard my own 'wrinkles as the roadmaps of my life.'"

– Renee Schreindl, Editor

"The desire to conspire, from one act of corruption to another, this real estate story puts you on the edge of your chair and in a state of disbelief. If your favorite genre is mystery, comedy, thriller or drama, this book is for you."

– Jeff Johns, eXp Realty

"As one of the karaoke stars the night at the old saloon, I shared many laughs with Ally and her family that weekend and throughout the duration of this book. I am finding out for the first time what truly happened behind closed doors and the strength she had to endure this roller coaster ride."

– Derek Heer, Friend

MAKE LEGAL U-TURN

WHEN NECESSARY

When a Move Out West Went South!

Allison J. Diedrick

Ten|16
PRESS

www.ten16press.com - Waukesha, WI

Written from the heart when the mind was overwhelmed

Change everything when everything changes

Reading between the lines of a real estate contract:
it's more than what meets the eye

Pure self-discovery of embracing God's plan for our lives

It is His wish for us to keep moving forward

The Lord is close to the brokenhearted
& saves those who are crushed in spirit.
Psalm 34:18

True life begins when you value yours and the lives of others

PREFACE

I credit my family and friends during a move that took me from Wisconsin to California and back again to Wisconsin. Thank you for throwing me a life jacket and not a heavy leather saddle. It was a bareback ride through California, and I think the fall knocked the wind out of me, so I needed more than a helping hand. I needed a movie director to appear out of nowhere and say, "Cut!" Or a voice to say, "Make legal U-turn when possible." There was no way I could have prepared myself for this move.

It truly was a series of unfortunate events, and I continue to ask myself, *is this fact or fiction*? But I will let you be the judge. Enjoy the read.

Warm Regards,

Allison J. Diedrick

I dedicate this book to:

My Parents

You literally gave me my legs to stand on and the world to conquer. Much like "The Man in the Arena" by Theodore Roosevelt, I am a fighter of principle, persevering even when the reflection in the mirror is of my own accord. The trials of this life are either attended to or ignored, and I would rather continue giving it my all, then placate to the few who are causing the disturbance. I live my life creatively and cherish the talents my mom and her mom gave me, and act upon them with tenacity, which comes from my dad. Before I could spell it, they were modeling it for me: CHARACTER!

My Sister

Without you and our 7:00 a.m. phone calls, I would have been on your doorstep Labor Day weekend 2015 until we moved in May 2017. Beyond the bond of sisterhood, I witnessed your professional nature comprised of exemplary service and knowledge obtained through your 30 years as a real estate broker in the state of California. Never compromising the integrity of a transaction or contract to suit a weighted party for personal gains. You are the best of the best!

My Sons

The ability to dream with the perseverance to obtain is the foundation upon which we built our family. Never give up! You both prevailed in the most difficult of times, at the most vulnerable times of your lives. Our world today revolves around the realization that miles do not add a void, love makes them voidable. We are mindfully present in each other's lives every single day regardless of the city, state, or country!

My Husband

For obvious reasons, I could not have written this book without you! Our humor combined with relentless badgering has kept us on our toes, and back in Wisconsin.

Better together defines our story. Twenty-eight years into this relationship, the flexibility and resiliency of our marriage has been stretched farther than I could have ever imagined, and I hope it continues!

I give this roller-coaster ride five stars. *****

The chapters are the journey, leaving you wanting more!

Chapter 1:
Please Sign In *W 1

Chapter 2:
Many Are Exhausted from the Energy in the Room *W 15

Chapter 3:
A Bushel and a Peck *W 22

Chapter 4:
Creative Talents *W 30

Chapter 5:
Even before the Move, This Is Not What I Had in Store *W 38

Chapter 6:
It's Beginning to Rain *W 46

Chapter 7:
For Sale by Owner *W 65

Chapter 8:
How to Live in the Wild Wild West *W 72

Chapter 9:
Instant Replay *C 81

Chapter 10:
House Hunting without a Gun *C 89

Chapter 11:
Re-loading *C 93

Chapter 12:
"Welcome!" Said the Spider to the Fly *C 100

Chapter 13:
Words That Begin with the Letter Z *C 105

Chapter 14:
Purchased with Heart *C 110

Chapter 15:
Four Eyes *C 114

Chapter 16:
Closing Day *C 120

Chapter 17:
Driving Home *C 127

Chapter 18:
24 hours in a Day *C 142

Chapter 19:
Batman and Robin *W 150

Chapter 20:
Poking the California Bear *C 160

Chapter 21:
Football Fool *C 173

Chapter 22:
Mediation or Plan Old Mediocrity *C 179

Chapter 23:
Westward Ho *W 185

Chapter 24:
Dixie to the Rescue *C 192

Chapter 25:
One Hell of a Rodeo *C 196

Chapter 26:
Karaoke at the Old Saloon *C 204

Chapter 27:
AD Troubles *C 211

Chapter 28:
Can You Win by Losing? *W 218

Chapter 29:
The Art of Finding JOY *W 244

*Chapters taking place in: *Wisconsin *California*

CHAPTER 1

Please Sign In

It's late October 2019 in Wisconsin, and it's snowing outside. The furnace in our 1930's lake home just kicked on, and the warm air is now reminiscent of just weeks ago when I had the windows open and the sun covered the house like a blanket. With the multitude of windows to look out of, I can see the snow masking everything I once knew to be. It looks as though someone is shaking a snow globe. And slowly, the picture outside my window is changing. A comfortable feeling on one hand, yet reflective of my life in California on the other.

Within two short years, California gave me a lifetime of experiences. And living happily was not one of them – it was more like living on the edge.

My brief stay in California was the sum of 648 days, less the 115 I spent self-imposed in the witness protection program. So 533 . . . less three nights spent in Northern California with my sister. My grand total is 530 days in Southern California. A place where if the sun doesn't burn you, the Department of Real Estate will. But let's talk about that later.

Before I get into the story, take a step back with me. Let me help you get to know me as best I can before I packed up and moved my life to follow someone else's.

A plain Jane description of your author: 5'1", red hair, freckles, brown eyes, married for 28 years and counting, mother of two, plus one puppy dog. Sibling to five others, middle child (though I may act like I am an only child at times). Slightly opinionated and incredibly intuitive, or vice versa. I have a heightened sense of awareness and a photographic memory. I'm a true believer of the law of attraction and the notion that what doesn't kill you makes you stronger (thank you, Kelly Clarkson).

For now, let's just simplify who I am and leave it as "complicated." It's not a secret that my life entails many entities, but there is one secret that I will have to whisper to you. It wasn't the law of attraction, it was the untold truth, what others knew and I did not. I could have overlooked it and moved on, or I could have pulled on all the strings that were raveled together into the words of this book.

And in this case, many strings, touched by many hands, weaved this story. Perhaps I was misled by a lack of experience and deceived by those who wished to acquire power by manipulation. I was their perfect target. At first I didn't know what was at the root of everything that happened, but I quickly learned it was people, power, lies, and corruption, and in the end, well, the end will leave you holding all the answers, and a false sense of security. I am sure everyone has a story to tell, but this four-year span in my life is not one that I ever intended on living or writing about. This story is the "secret" that I have been keeping. If you wondered what I was doing in California, you're not alone. I was wondering that too, but now after writing this book, you, along with everyone else, will know the story. And if by chance you knew me before I left as Ally or By Ally, you just became my Ally-by (alibi).

I have always seen myself as an individual who self-energizes, tires others out, and loves being in control of what I am doing and what others intend to do. A fireball at times. It's never a dull moment when I am with others I know well, primarily my family, or even when I'm just by myself. Of course, if we had just met, I wouldn't really let the Ally Cat out of the bag – fully exposing my true self. It's more of a slow pounce, exposing my personality slowly so it doesn't knock you off your feet. In new social circles, I am much more reticent, absorbing the aura around me. And in California, the social circles ironically circled around families. Inviting me in, but truly leaving me out. Is it the old saying, "Keep your friends close, and your enemies closer"? I'm not sure, but let's just go with that!

I align myself with the chameleon, blending in or quickly departing, and I am completely comfortable with that. An Irish goodbye at times also fits my character. My favorite morning ritual is looking in the mirror and preparing myself for whatever the reflection reveals – sometimes the stare back is "Oh no, not you again." That's truly one thing about being creative, it's never dull. Each day isn't just planned to accommodate the priorities, it includes spontaneous diversions of unplanned projects, whirlwind adventures, and unorganized and organized chaos. Maybe somedays it's form over function, and others function over form.

But generally, every day includes a little routine of the natural order, starting with a little domestic housework, but often ending atypical in nature. I can equally exchange a cookie cutter for a handheld jigsaw, or electric knife for a circular saw. A pastry tube for a grout bag, or even a router. The excitement of taking a kitchen gadget and making it a workshop tool and vice versa is unexplained unless you give it a whirl on your own. A trip to the hardware store is far more interesting, as well as distracting, than the average trip to the grocery store. At the hardware store, the end caps are as exciting as the aisles, and the possibilities are endless, as well as calorie-free. Creating a recipe can happen at either location, and an apron is appropriate for both.

My wardrobe changed as my talents developed, and new discoveries were made. Paint, for instance, is truly much more difficult to get out of blouses and pants than tomato sauce and mustard. I also have had the challenge on several occasions of trying to clean a gallon of paint out of my car, and another car that did not belong to me. It somewhat resembled a Mercedes wagon with a full bag of golf clubs which belonged to a very close relative, and let's leave it at that. That's another mystery.

Changing clothes throughout the day never enticed me, nor did opening paint cans with an apron on. Perhaps this is just another attribute to my character: I am a little colorful at times. I'm also a little weak when hammering the lids on to create a no-spill seal, hence the episode with the golf clubs. I also didn't see wearing an apron in the workshop as glamorous or as nostalgic as wearing an apron in the kitchen. Donna Reed from *It's a Wonderful Life* and Barbara Billingsley, known as June Cleaver on *Leave It to Beaver*, both wore aprons along with their high heels, dresses, lipstick, and perfectly "molded" hair from heavy hairspray. I just love that look, and though I've never duplicated it, it's truly on my bucket list. To wake up, put on a dress, and waltz around the house all day and not get messy seems incredibly interesting to me. Boring, perhaps, but interesting. As a little girl, I loved wearing my mom's high heels, and I preferred the blue pair with the gold buckle and chunky heels, which aided in my ability to shuffle along without the extreme balancing act. I also admired her straw purse with brown leather handles and a clasp of gold. It wasn't one you carried over your shoulder, but in your hand. The memories of my bare feet in her shoes, shuffling across the green shag carpet while holding her purse, are moments in time I hope to never forget. It was that "classic look" she bestowed onto me which I try to emulate today.

I'd also love to live a week in the life of *I Dream of Jeannie*. But do not misunderstand, I do not want to copy Barbara Eden's look, or call my spouse "Master," I just want to blink and have things appear or disappear. I already have the ponytail, and I have had lots of practice folding my arms, so I believe I am ready. I love taking immediate action to whatever I want to achieve and enjoy helping others with the same. Perhaps, like Jeannie's character, I am an extreme people-pleaser. I want to engage in activities and keep energy moving forward rather than burning energy while standing still. I am goal-oriented and love to accomplish as much as possible in any given day. In today's world, no matter how much we've planned, and even when we think we have it all together, $h?t can hit the fan. I wasn't wearing an apron when we moved, and in hindsight, I should have. Maybe even a hazmat outfit.

True, I have sewn numerous denim aprons, mostly to sell, or for the benefit of wearing one with pockets during a craft sale. The infamous Holiday Sale which took place in my Pewaukee house garage usually called for a layering of clothing which I would top off with a knee-length denim apron. Perfect for extra warmth because this outdoor event generally took place right around Thanksgiving. I would purposely keep the garage door down until the last possible minute, for once it opened, the brisk air chilled you to the bone and the cold concrete floor felt as though you were walking on ice. I remember a very chilly Friday evening, a good friend and her husband, whom I had never met, stopped over to preview the sale. Both were dressed in black leather jackets, headed to or coming from a Friday Fish Fry. My girlfriend had on ankle boots, and her husband, black braided tassel loafers. You know the kind; the soles offer no insulation, and neither do the socks. As they walked around the garage, I could see the cold, raw concrete floor turning their feet into blocks of ice. Along with the numbing of their feet, the cold garage turned their noses candy apple red! I couldn't tell from the dimly lit garage if their smiles were frozen, or if in fact their lips were holding their teeth from chattering. But in an instant, they were purchasing everything from florals to holiday décor; sales were heating up, and the cold hard cash was warming my pockets. The good doctor, and husband to my friend, later became one of my husband's biking buddies. And my friend, well, I think she convinced me that evening, without saying a word, that opening a store should be something I should consider.

I designed and wore an apron on a Fox 6 News midmorning segment, *How to Prepare a Meal for 4 for under $10.00*. The apron was a transformed dress shirt that once belonged to my older son, and it allowed for an iPod, thermometer, hand towel, and had a collar to complete the look. The meal I whipped up was Sweet Salsa Chicken. I practiced that meal for a week, and night after night, my family happily ate it. The designer apron along with the entrée became infamous at our house. After the TV appearance, I seldom wore the apron, since I didn't want to spill anything on it. An oxymoron, I guess. My kids often asked how I secured that appearance. My response was simple. I was listening to the radio in the garage, between the air compressor refilling and the sound of the staple gun shooting staples into a cornice board I was fabricating. I heard the advertisement and immediately stopped what I was doing, went into the house, called the studio, and basically said to them, "I could do that!" And so, I did. Perhaps it was the challenge of creating the meal, for I had no idea what the meal would be, or perhaps it was the desire to use my hotel restaurant management degree. Either way, I found myself gearing up for being on TV and whipping up a recipe that would be delicious and affordable.

I often wonder, if I had heard an advertisement on the radio inviting me to move to California, would I have had the same "Yes, I can do that" reaction? No, I think not, accompanied with a sanguine smile. I've vacationed numerous times in California, but always enjoyed returning home to Wisconsin.

Moving around the kitchen is one thing, but moving to what felt like halfway around the world? Well, I am sure I would have spewed laughter right along with the staples being thrown from the gun. Yet years later, it wasn't a commercial on the radio, it was live. And I didn't really know that I needed more than an apron, I needed a spacesuit, because the story is completely out of this world. And as I desperately try to describe me before California, I've purposely backtracked to the days of "Mayberry," otherwise known as Chilton, and later Pewaukee, WI. Ron Howard, I hope you read this book, I would love a Sheriff Andy reply to this madness.

As the years passed, decorating truly became my passion. My perception of the value of what I was wearing didn't hold a candle to what I was putting on walls, windows, shelves, chairs, and so on. Paint became my initial focus, and if it just so happened to land on the Cabi garments I was wearing that day, oh well. I didn't see what the problem was, but my husband did. Not impressed with several of my outfits that I would try to wear out in public, he eventually threw them out. My favorite jeans disappeared, along with several jackets, t-shirts, blouses, and so on. My kids started to notice their clothing also took on added color. And soon, instead of looking for something to wear, piles of unwanted clothes appeared on my bed. I think that was to safeguard what they didn't want me to wear.

A local hardware store employee commented one day, yelling out, "Hey, Picasso, do you ever get any paint on the walls?" In this case, I loved the humor, but not so much at another business when it was suggested that I head to the back of the store where the discounted furniture pieces were located. And at another store, an employee asked me, "Is the paint dry on your clothes before you touch the fabrics?" Yes, painting is messy. And if the law of attraction applies, it certainly applied here. I couldn't open a paint lid without immediately wearing the color. The harder I would try to stay paint-free, the more it gravitated to whatever I was sporting that day. A simple touch-up became a vast deluge of color somewhere on me. Hard to believe, but I loved it. The colors, for the most part, were those I had suggested for my clients, and the memories from each marking, well, that made many of my garments priceless! On numerous occasions when I have been out shopping, people would ask where I got my painted pants, and my reply was, "They're originals." I was a walking billboard. To this day, I still sport a jacket my grandmother Sally gave me. It's a London Fog short raincoat, tan in color with plaid lining, a sure classic. I love everything about it! It's the little jacket that our "height" matched perfectly with. Even with a little green paint on the cuff that I did not intend to add, it is still very much my favorite! Our family has sported many items splashed with paint, and I think over the years, we all have come to realize that creativity happens instantly, and there is no time to change outfits between thought and action. And, as colorful and creative as I thought I was, I thought I also had the go-with-the-flow attitude and was living an abundant life. If it was broken, I had the attitude that I could fix it, and if something was "shabby" I could make it "chic!" I don't know what California was to me, other than it wasn't! So, I will stay the course, and keep you on track with my life as I once knew it to be.

Simply put, I was in control. Just humming along on a two-way highway without the need for a crash helmet, brakes, or U-turn for that matter. Country roads and farm stands as far as the eye could see. Art manifested into the love of gardening, cooking, baking, and canning, a tradition my mom passed on to me. Pickled beets along with a garden relish are my absolute favorites. If you want to pick a beautiful paint color for your house, walk into a garden – floral or vegetable. Seriously, the color palette is unlike any other. The shades and hues of flowers along with the robust colors of fruits and vegetables are perfect for the plate and the palette. For the plate, traditional holiday gatherings call for delicious traditional eats. All colors balanced to create the perfect meal. And when garden colors portray paint colors, the bold and the beautiful tell a story, and the soft and pastel transcend into new beginnings and land themselves into nurseries. As a decorator, I believe you should be the narrator of your home. Let your color selections tell your story. And in my case, my role of decorator and homeowner intertwine. I tend to be adventurous in the kitchen and have deviated from the traditional role when compared to my mom. My kitchen projects are centered around more than just food. For instance, sipping high voltage caffeinated coffee in the morning or tea in the afternoon in the kitchen is paired perfectly with sewing or painting canvas pieces at the island or kitchen table. I have often made my kitchen my studio, working on all types of projects that probably should have been re-routed to the garage or basement.

But as time progressed, so did the education process. I did happen to notice that not all projects were suitable for the kitchen. Paint is very difficult to get off laminate flooring, and nails that penetrate wood also can penetrate laminate countertops. On the bright side, however, this truly ruled as a double win for me, for I ordered Brazilian cherry wood floors along with granite countertops.

An amazingly funny story that I must quickly share. It was November, winter weather was upon us, and the decision to remodel pulled at my heartstrings. So, I ordered the Brazilian cherry wood floors, measured for the granite, picked out the new sink and faucet, and selected the carpet. One night after work, my husband Keith walked into the house and noticed a load of wood in our living room and asked, "What's that for?" I couldn't quite tell if he was seriously asking me this question, or if he was really hoping for the response to be that we were just storing it for a client. I confidently replied, "We are installing hardwood this week, but the wood needs to come to temperature. But don't worry about that. The sink, faucet, and granite will be installed tomorrow, followed by the hardwood installation, and lastly the carpet will arrive." Of course, this flowed out of my mouth followed by a big smile. Everything was under control, except for a little inconvenience that week of crawling through the living room window when leaving or entering the house. Both entrances to the home were basically under construction. From staining to sealing, the off-limits had all of us off-roading. We all had to improvise, and we did. At my personal height of five feet tall, thank goodness there was a deck to first step onto before trying to climb through the window. This so-called "hurdle" enlisted our family of five, which included our Airedale, Marlo, to literally have to jump through hoops. A sight to be seen I'm sure.

And did I say November? Yes, November. Snow and cold and Thanksgiving was soon happening at our house. So, onto the next project or, in my case, projects. Preparing the holiday meal also incorporated simple projects between basting the turkey and boiling the potatoes.

Again, why so much information about your author? I'm trying wholeheartedly to give you my background because as we move forward, I lost myself in the story of "unbelievable happenings." No one knew me, no one believed me, and there I sat, dumbfounded that this could really happen. This is unlike any movie, or episode of the Jerry Springer show. But wait, could it be? All I know is I didn't appreciate how much I loved my life until I didn't. My incredibly energized life started to tank the closer I got to the shores of the Pacific Ocean, but once we truly arrived, the tow started pulling me under.

CHAPTER 2

Many Are Exhausted from the Energy in the Room

"Be still in the moment" never worked for me. I love to make a daily task list that sometimes requires two pages. I navigate by landmarks (hence the many routes I have discovered to get to Muskego to see George and Jayne). I tend to have the most current electronic devices thanks to my husband but lack the knowledge on how to use them. I exhaust my kids with questions, and, reluctantly at times, they sit me down for a remedial course. I still haven't grasped how to hold my cell phone according to my younger son Cal – something about using my thumb. One technical difficulty I share with my devices is I rarely plug them in to recharge. Ironically, the charger is never where I left it, and the mysterious disappearance also includes an empty gas tank.

Without the car charger, and with a notorious low battery on my phone, I navigate through my day encountering road closures, alternative routes, orange barrels, and rummage sales. In Wisconsin, the orange barrels appear when the state bird returns announcing that summer is coming. And rummage sales are pure distractions, which cause my car to veer off into driveways in hopes of seeking treasures, according to my older son Kevin. What was California going to bring? Six lanes of traffic in each direction. Along with the possibility that each individual lane would take me somewhere I didn't want to go. Trouble navigating just multiplied.

I was nicknamed "Radar" when I was younger, which depicted my keen ability to hear, see, and respond to things that were not necessarily intended for me. Growing up with five siblings and placing myself in the middle always kept me alert, wide-eyed, and ears perked. Perhaps the gigantic slippery slide at an amusement park stretched my eyes on the upward climb and on the downward travel. And my notorious short hair, never over the ear, aided in my keen sense of hearing. Whatever the case, I did not implore those talents earlier in my life by becoming a detective, but I have recently included them in my repertoire along with gun safety and how to operate a security system. I have never been a fan of scary movies or those without happy endings. If it's going to be a mystery read, it better be a Nancy Drew, and if I had to pick a favorite detective, it would be Angela Lansbury's character, Jessica Fletcher. She may have worn a trench coat, but I believe it was because it was going to rain. She refrained from the dark sunglasses and hat, which made her persona even more mysterious because she replaced her exterior look with interior perception. She was brave, motherly, and delightful. However, prior to my California arrival, I thought I had the Doris Day look going for myself. Happy, funny, and adventurous. And if we stick with the Doris Day theme for a moment longer, when we departed California, the movie *With Six You Get Eggroll* with Brian Keith depicts it best. Doris is driving a pickup truck with a camper overhead, and Brian Keith is in the back looking through the window as if yelling, "Honey, please slow down!" Yes, this clearly describes the look of our drive home. To get the visual, please Google it. It's priceless.

Keeping it real is difficult, keeping it simple is complicated, and considering myself anything but normal is safe. By the way, what is normal? I am a procrastinator just by being creative. I cannot start a project until I have visualized the end result. And if the end result is not what I had envisioned, well, I would have to **start completely over!** – fastidious perhaps. Now combine that with a little attention deficit disorder or the urge to multitask, and you end up with how I see the day. Intuitively "defined" with an overabundance of options! Believe it or not, it's true. I have found that if I try to focus on just one thing,

I spend my day feeling sluggish and tired. When I have a whirlwind of a day, I am most productive, but everyone else is tired.

Lately I have been fixated on the sense that most of the world does not operate like this. I often find myself asking the question, "What do they do all day?" California provoked additional questions, and of course offered unsolicited advice. Like I've mentioned, I was experienced in vacationing in California, say over nine trips, though it never got easier. And like California, New York, Mexico, South Dakota, Maryland, England, and on and on, they all have stories to tell. I think I have expectations that are so incredibly high that it translates into disappointment. Which is why my older son always tells me, "If you would just lower your expectations, you would be a lot happier." I will never forget that line.

My à la carte list of what defines me is as long as the list of goals that I want to achieve each day. Some may find this to be exhausting, but I have always thought it to be challenging. The challenge begins each morning, and seriously, if I can get at least five to six hours of restful sleep, I am programed to take on the world and all its challenges. If sleep escapes me, it takes me about an hour in the morning to reboot. Coffee, a clean house, and a clean car energizes me. I am quite self-aware, and to a degree, its side effect is I'm quite self-aware. I do tend to judge myself even before others have a chance. When Kevin told me if I just lowered my expectations, I would be happier, I think he meant the people around me would be happier, and I would certainly have to agree with that. I also have been told that I repeat myself. Ha, but in theory, what we repeat is often what we are focusing on.

On an episode of *The Real Housewives of Orange County,* someone once said, "Don't smile, it causes wrinkles." Well, in that case, I was onto something. In California, I rarely smiled. I cried a lot. My skin should have thanked me, for a neighbor recently told me that the natural saline in tears clears up skin blemishes. I guess I didn't have any blemishes, just the start of RBF, and I haven't quite discovered the cure for that. But more than tears, living in California ultimately affected my sense of well-being and damaged my heart and soul. I wasn't *living* in California, I was *surviving.*

Today, I am finding myself racing into the wind to keep the wrinkles away, and it's only when I'm standing still that I really notice them. I call them my road maps, depicting the contours of my life and the many directions I have taken.

I am a people-pleaser by nature and value other's opinions. I also like to share my own thoughts and prefer everyone to agree with them. As my dad explained to me, I like to play by the rules, but I make a lot of them up as I go. I am classified as an excellent backseat driver. When you are driving, I will assist you by calling out "Brake!" when needed, or simply use body movements by holding the dash or grabbing the handle. Cars are my thing, more so than diamonds, and the color white is my favorite, right along with another form of transportation, my flip flops. Hard on my back, but the name is so perfect, and funny. The natural elements also affect their function. Rain makes them slip flops, and wearing them in winter makes for a broken leg. Close call, but I regained my composure by grabbing the door handle of the minivan. Early morning coffee runs through a local drive-through coffee shop presented this opportunity, where it seemed faster to slip on flip flops than boots. So, between a clean house and a clean white car, cozy pajamas, flip flops, and a cup of coffee, any day can be a holiday.

Each day I see as a gift from God, and how I use it is the gift I give back to Him. I am not trying to run a race with my life, but I am trying to find what I am here for. I have been told that we have over 500-800 talents to explore within each of us, so part of me is on a mission to find out what they are. I have noticed more of my faults recently than my talents, for it seems all my juggling has turned into a pile of broken plates. But on the flipside, I have had time to conjure up one new interest, and that entailed writing this book. A bucket list idea that never made it to paper until now. At least I can tell you that I have never devoted this much time to any college assignment or high school English essay ever!

I still feel childlike, and that sense of wonder is still around me. But what has changed is the clarity that bad things can happen to good people. This experience I am about to share isn't the worst thing to have happened in the entire world, but it personally shook *my* world. Moving to California had been an adventure, living there a nightmare, and moving back a blessing!

CHAPTER 3

A Bushel and a Peck

Now that you have begun to understand me, everything seemed to be great in Wisconsin until my apple cart overturned and apples (life routines) rolled in every possible direction. A sibling described this visual for me while we were on the phone one day, and it really sunk in. I felt like it was the end-all of a perfect life I created. Literally my roots were being pulled up and I was being transplanted to a state without any water. At least that is how the news showcased the state of California. And it mimicked how I was feeling. I wasn't prepared for change, nor for a drought, in any aspect of my life. I was still actively making it all happen. I had finally just opened my own store and was pursuing my dreams. My life was full and lush and green. And I was totally unprepared for a drought. The state of California mandated the reduction of watering lawns, washing cars in the driveway, and personal use in the home. A desert state, with hot, dry days, could only lead to more freckles or a permanent sunburn. I rarely tanned in Wisconsin. And the rotation of burn, peel, and repeat didn't intrigue me.

I couldn't even imagine what it was going to be like living in the desert with heat upwards of 110 degrees. I tried the self-tanning products and usually ended up with streaks, spots, and orange clothing. The worst, however, was a very memorable vacation we took to California years prior to the move. We vacationed at Newport Coast Villas with my sister's family. The weather was sunny that day, but the air was cool and somewhat cloudy. New to the area and still naïve to my older sister's recommendations, Kate told me to go to the room and get a green bottle from the counter. When I returned to the pool, she said, "Put it on," and so I did. And I laid in the sun all day. What a great start to the vacation. I ended up with orange hands and orange, baked skin which resembled a sweet potato. The lotion was self-tanning, not sunblock. The pain chart, normally a 0-10, took me over 20. Poolside lounging moved to bedside moaning. I did manage to move again by the third day and went to the salon for a great, short haircut unlike any other. Unfortunately, my moment of happiness diverted quickly to a hair dryer burn on my neck – deepening the sweet potato to a tomato color. Vacationing always sounds exciting to me but leaves me feeling anxious. I think I pack far too many expectations than I could ever carry. And that becomes my demise. Even as the calendar days progress to the date of departure, I inadvertently misplace the airline tickets, lose my license, and often misplace my iPod or purse. Yet, I am great at booking the tickets, suggesting what type of rental car, and I enjoy the thought of getting away. But as reality revealed the truth, it never went as planned. It's been discovered by many that it is best to send me three days in advance, for there is an adjustment period I need to go through in order for everyone else to enjoy their trip. Perhaps the overturned apple cart was my own way of discovering that I am a complete and utmost creature of habit, and why change is extremely difficult for me.

Whatever the case, the overturned cart contained my life, and it spilled out all over the place when my husband asked us to move to California for his job. My faith, family, friends, social groups, house, business, hobbies, fitness program, family coordinator, garden keeper, flower bed tender, project manager, and "me" rolled uncontrollably all over. An incredible disparity of a chin-dragging, heart-deflating episode of "What the hell?" Sleepless nights, restless days, and tears of all kinds. Tears of joy one moment, fear the next, happiness, sadness, excitement, and of course tears from onions – meals still had to be made. If I cried, somedays the storm would pass as natural as a warm summer rain. And other times, between the thunder and lightning, tantrums and sparks flying off my tongue through the phone, I would somehow decompress, regain my stamina to continue, and start again. In theory, I got a divorce every other day. I drafted up a divorce settlement, and it included a Mercedes every three years along with all sorts of goodies, but that too seemed like a miserable road to travel down, no matter what mode of transportation. And when Keith agreed to whatever my demands were, it wasn't as exciting. And no car or sum of money could replace the memories together or the time apart, and I knew if I focused on the "I will never be able to make this up to you," it could play into great benefits, but that is not what makes up a relationship.

This transition in life involved more than just moving. I was aging, and soon becoming an empty nester, and it all came at once. This whole ordeal was like a favorite line from a Jason Aldean song; it was "pedal to the metal on a downhill slide." No brakes, barriers, or bunkers. My apples were rolling down a hill faster than I could follow, and my apron strings couldn't stretch any further. My faith couldn't hold the momentum back, and lack of faith couldn't move me forward. I was stuck. I had once heard that you cannot have faith and doubt at the same time, but let's be honest, and add uniqueness to my character, I think I mastered both. Faith got me up each morning, and doubt fell upon me each night. My Facebook friends eased the pain of departure and traveled with me each mile. If I posted and they "liked" it, I was smooth sailing for at least a hundred miles. The house I just sold was decorated with love, and I knew I could do it again regardless of my bad attitude of "nope" and "not going to happen." My talents were basically my hobbies, and if I wanted to open another store, well, the population in California could certainly support it. Thirty-eight million people and counting, for three more were moving in. And honestly, if I wanted to continue to work out, the warm weather and the scenery would be perfect for it. I knew there had to be a reason why every apple rolled, but each day I somehow ended with negative reasoning. My vocabulary evolved, and my patience dwindled. Did I mention that Keith moved a year and half before me? If not, I will get to it later. He also moved back nine months before me. And yes, we are still married.

I love to engage in exercise but happen to have an all-in or all-out attitude. Two years prior to our move, I was a certified group fitness instructor, setting the bar high enough for all to get an honest workout, always accompanied by music which would pump you up and also drove up Keith's iTunes account. Personally speaking, music can motivate, calm, or take me down memory lane. Yet, like a dumbbell, I dropped the habit and picked up the weight (if you know what I mean) when I found out about our move. I stopped listening to music, and I stopped working out. I let go of an important element that nurtures us in times of stress, relaxes us in times of tension, and soothes us mentally in times of despair.

Your body will thank you when you work out and cause you grief when you don't. The latter happened, and that void in my life became obvious. Have you ever watched the movie *Legally Blonde*? "Endorphins make you happy, and happy people don't kill their husbands." I didn't have any endorphins, and luckily for my husband, he was in another state. But without working out, any optimism I did have was heading south, while my fatigue was heading north. Have you ever considered the spelling resemblance between fat-i-gue and Fat I go? Trust me, I lived it. If you don't exercise and eat right, stress and fatigue will weigh you down. The change was out of my control, and I was a deer in the headlights.

The thought of moving was killing me, and if I would have known the experience itself was going to be this difficult, I would have started this book years ago, for it would have been a great way to document my sanity while I still had it. My initial book title was *And then . . . More $h?t Happened*. But before moving too far ahead, I must give credit to the person who *inspired* the original title, and moved my cheese, and literally this time, Keith. Ironically, around the time of our move out of the dairy state, I found myself to be more lactose intolerant. Was it a sign of age, or was it keeping up with the times and changing with the trends? I don't recall my parents or grandparents experiencing any food allergies. Almond milk is my dairy replacement, and here is where my creativity comes into play. I have an incredible ability to be distracted. So here goes . . . Why hasn't Dairy Queen invented an Almond King cone? Picture this: a gluten-free waffle cone dipped in chocolate (chocolate with cannabis in California . . .) rolled in slivered almonds and filled with soft-serve almond milk? I can see it, can't you? The problem is I want to taste it!

This interjection of a creative idea for me is an everyday common occurrence. And moving me out of the state, to a state where they have "happy cows"? Are you kidding me? The grass isn't always greener on the other side – California was in a state of drought.

What transpired in California was a spicy concoction which gave me acid reflux and indigestion, high blood pressure, weight gain, stress, anxiety, and an unfavorable look at my future. One would think that living in a sunny state would recharge your battery, like being solar-powered; however, this was not the case. I felt like the state depleted my energy. I thought shaking up my life would be great, but as my dad once told me, "The more you do, the more you will experience, good and bad." Well, I find myself doing a lot more than the average Jane. (Sorry, Joe, but Jane's my middle name, and the odds seemed so much "riskier" at my age.) And I knew I must have been on the brink of the 80/20 rule. Eighty percent of what I encountered left me with only 20 percent happiness. What the hell? Change has never been part of my vocabulary, even though the word "decorating" is. And decorating is what I loved to do, but I wasn't quite feeling it in Norco, California. I was feeling compelled to become a private investigator, a lawyer, or a divorcee. Yes, I truly considered all three. How could it be that I had this nice little life going, a history of happiness with a passion for decorating, and ended up in a state of misery? Perhaps it is true, people have suitcases full of their past experiences, and as I started packing mine for the move, I realized I couldn't get them closed. I was overpacking, eagerly trying to take my history with me.

CHAPTER 4

Creative Talents

    I started decorating with my mom in the early '90s, and we called ourselves "The Greatvine Crafters." Together, we crafted holiday pieces that we would showcase at local craft shows, and many of the items were made of handpicked grapevines. My mom is extremely talented. I favored her skills, and her talents inspired me. She is an amazing woman who raised six children with six unique personalities and believed each of us could conquer the world if we had it in our heart and soul to do so. So, there was no one better to venture out into the craft world with, no other but my mom. The two of us created and crafted up a storm, our apron strings knotted together. And my acknowledgement that I needed a bigger car became apparent when making an autumn delivery of crafts to an apple farm.

My white Mitsubishi Diamante could not hold any more than what was already inside. I had my mom, my Grandma Sally, and my two babes, along with all our crafts. It was when I was pulling up to the barn to unload that I realized I needed a minivan. Everyone was too precious for me to leave home, and everyone looked too squished to be comfy, except for me, the driver, of course. But looking in the rearview mirror, the look on my grandmother's face was priceless. She was sitting in the back seat snuggled between her great-grandchildren in car seats, with a floral arrangement on her lap and very close to having a decorated grapevine wreath around her neck. I could also see her halo over her head, smiling and as happy as one could be. And at that very moment, a memory was created to last a lifetime.

Soon thereafter, the children's song "The Wheels on the Bus Go Round and Round" turned into a minivan rolling down the country roads with comfortable seating for everyone, including my grandmother, and space for crafts, sippy cups, pretzels, diaper bags, strollers, and anything else needed. And as the grapevines continued to grow, so did the business. We ventured out from grapevines and created everything from hand-painted t-shirts, to artistic tiles created on corkboards to hang on walls, to in-home party shows. My sister-in-law Gina hosted the first in-home décor party, and from there I was off to our local parks and recreation department selling and teaching classes. All of this became an extension of what began as a hobby called Greatvine Crafters and evolved into a new business and soon to a storefront. Gallon after gallon of paint rolled onto walls, along with numerous faux finishes creating the look of wallpaper but better, no mess or paste to deal with. I had the good fortune of working with a neighbor, who taught me so much more than just staying up late to craft and how to tie a bow. She shared in the passion of doing what you love, but more importantly, doing it while expressing one's own identity. Incredibly brave and multitalented, she was my version of a woman who had it all together. No better day was spent than one when we would paint, entertain each other, and laugh until we cried. And our reward at the end of the day would be to head to PDQ for a muffin and a coffee. And yes, it was true; we were "Pretty Damn Quick" painters and enjoyed many muffins and coffees together!

From crafting, I moved on to murals and floral gardens which grew from tubes of paint and birdhouses, and bird benches were built from pine boards and reclaimed wood. I started to recruit help and connected with talented "heart-ists." Lamps were made of clay pots and antique canning jars as well as birdhouses, and on one day, a barn lamp was ordered with operating doors. If I had a vision, I had special people in my life making it happen, including my husband. Thursday evenings at our house were called "all-night Thursday nights," and we would work into the wee hours of the morning. If the project didn't require my husband, his presence still made the difference. He would watch TV or sleep on occasion, sometimes both at the same time. Hmmm, he and Dad have something in common. My dad was infamous for that. Growing up, Sundays for sure, my dad would turn on the football game and at the same time have a newspaper laying over his face. I would turn the channel thinking he was sleeping, and he would respond with, "Hey, I was watching that!" Incredibly talented I tell you; sleeping, watching TV, and reading the paper all at once simply amazed me. And falling into a new craft or experimenting in the kitchen was perfect for football season. There was never an interruption from my family. They were all focused on the game, and I on my craft. I could pull out the sewing machine my parents had given me as a Christmas gift in 1991 and stitch my way through hot pads, aprons, tree skirts, window treatments, bedding, pillows, and light upholstery work. I still use that same machine today, accompanied by four others. Initially, I started out sewing apparel, and I can vividly recall a blouse I made for my mom's mom, my sweet Grandma Elsie. It was complete with tiny covered buttons and a mandarin collar, and she wore it to dinner one evening at our house. It was one of my biggest thrills as I sat across from her admiring her caramel-colored blouse patterned with small green, gold, teal, and orange leaves. She coordinated it perfectly with her brown slacks. She had rosy red cheeks, a dainty frame, and a smile that would warm your heart. She called me her little "Allie Kins," and I loved it. We would fish together, pick hickory nuts, and sometimes attend four o'clock mass together at Saint Augustine's Church. She would say her rosary and taught her bird Ernie to do the same. She was an amazing woman. One of the first women in her hometown to wear blue jeans and a jean jacket. Talented artistically, as well as domestically, she was a baker, seamstress, and loved a tidy home and yard. She exhibited confidence! I started sewing everything from a swimming suit, to pants worn by my sister and college roommate, to maternity clothes, and my children's clothes. One project that didn't quite make the cut however was a blue corduroy jacket for my dad, complete with shoulder pads, leather buttons, and false pockets. It seemed to have taken months and was an all-out disaster as well as out of style by the time I finished, but I finished.

My "happiness" grew with the excitement of my clients and the referrals they provided me. And as my business grew, so did my creative interests. The first piece of furniture I painted came from Illinois; the door of the truck opened, and out came a gallon of paint. The headboard and footboard, made of maple and stained to last a lifetime, lapped up the creamy white paint and was soon sold to a friend. Ottomans became a need for everyone, and my aunt cut the wood and created the frames while I secured the foam and did the upholstery work. The possibilities of what to do next seemed endless. Each new home challenged me and gave me the opportunity to explore unique and innovative ways to distinguish their home, inclusive of their style and how they chose to live, comfort always being the key factor.

I am a toe tapper, and my lack of patience equates to, I'm sure, a lack of patients. I was only referenced as Dr. Décor when playing sheepshead online. Somewhere between Grassy Hill and Baa, I was booted off, and without any patience, it was my last time. I declined to re-join and took my available spare time back into the workshop, so it must have been October. It was the month to pull grapevines. I am the "deck the halls in the middle of summer" type of gal; I play holiday movies starting in late September and October. Staying ahead of my competition has always been my goal, whether as a storeowner or in my own home. I am not a Pinterest or Etsy person; I would prefer to BE the competition and not chase it. But ironically today, I own Pinterest stock.

Starting the holidays off early is like running a race, and because I am not really a runner, any advantage to stay ahead of the game works for me. So, from this little intro, you may see that I am a little competitive, but please don't let me put words in your mouth. However, I will put food in your mouth. I love to cook, hate to grocery shop, and am good at making a reservation.

I have never sat still long enough for paint to dry, an engine to cool, or an alarm clock to go off. And for that reason, I've preferred not to use oil-based paints or stains. I have a difficult time coloring within the lines, so adult coloring books stress me out! I have not sat long enough to pick up the art of crocheting or knitting, but one Christmas I did receive a loom from my parents to make scarves, and I loved it, and still have it. It allowed me to master the art of multitasking at an early age. I could watch TV, work the loom, and carry on a conversation at the age of eight. I did try cross-stitch once while being a passenger in a car and couldn't follow the pattern just like I can't follow a map. I have always set my own course, "self-guided adventures" if you will. But what truly motivates me is I love people and I love art and I love to make people happy! Taking the entrepreneurial route bonded me with my dad, and working beside my mom in the kitchen bonded me with her, apron strings and all. My original dream in high school was to have a house, six kids, a paneled station wagon, and a dog, which, ironically, was everything my mom had. My dad said no to that and told me I needed to go to college. He has been my mentor all my life. I believe I have exactly the parents God intended me to have to be the person I am. That describes your author – Me! And if you are thinking "Hurry up and get to the real story," well, this is part of it. These chapters became the reasons, not the excuses, that I didn't want to leave the state.

My focus on life as it was seemed better than it was ever going to be, so just like my life and story moving forward, there is a delay. I have purposely outlined my character for you simply by validating me. And if you never believe the rest of the story, or even if you do, prepare to hold on. You are almost there, the storm is just creeping in. When someone suggests a storm is creeping in, the need for an umbrella sounds logical, along with rain boots or even snow boots for that matter. But what I really needed to continue wearing moving forward was my apron. Providing an extra layer of protection, covering my heart.

CHAPTER 5

Even before the Move, This Is Not What I Had in Store

2011 and 2012 were somewhat turbulent years. It started when I connected with another woman who also dreamt of owning a storefront. At a local coffee shop, I sat in a booth across from a client, sipping coffee and listening to her dreams of opening a storefront. She had recently retired and was fully open to any opportunities. I drank my coffee black, so there was no cream or sugar to coat the conversation, only a hot liquid flowing down my throat, drowning a very goal of my own. She asked for my help, and I was hooked. My brain kicked into "What can I do for you?" And someone wanting my creativity at a storefront level sweetened the coffee, and I spilled the ideas. My first offer was to be a consultant, selling my skillset. But she said no, she couldn't afford a consultant. Puzzled, I stared back into her eyes. What is she not telling me? Wait, she wants me to be her decorator? What??? I was confused, but flattered. Reckless with my business plan, I accepted her invitation to help her. We met as a foursome, spouses included. A contract was drawn up, inclusive of non-use of my secure vendor list, which had taken me 20 years to compile.

I worked at the store and had the opportunity to bring in my creations – painted furniture, a specialty of mine. In addition, I said I would paint the exterior storefront with faux stone, pick the interior colors, and work for free. I was to be paid a commission when my pieces sold and was responsible for having inventory to replace units as they sold. So far, so good, I guess. I had been cultivating my talent for the last 20-plus years, and yes, my painted furniture pieces were flying out of the store. Success can bring envy, and envy brought in enmity. I was told I was going to be competing with another furniture painter. One evening I called a contractor that I had been working with to assist me in the morning with the unloading of furniture pieces the store owner wanted, not only to add to the store floor, but to start accumulating as backup in a storage area. The alley was narrow and had only one way in and out. But there stood my contractor, ready to help me unload. And as we carried the first heavy piece to the showroom, I collapsed from the weight of my own heart. The store was flooded with items from my number one vendor – flowers, stems, arrangements, and décor all from my secured wholesale provider. All I could fathom at this moment was the educator was the hardest to educate. I pulled my inventory and turned my direction towards home. This incredible experience didn't change my decision to open a store, it re-routed me. I made a legal U-turn and proceeded towards my goal.

I always thought, since my dad was a real estate broker and owned several car dealerships, that I was named after the Allison Transmission, hence *For the Long Haul*. However, I do recall an ice-skating event that doesn't quite fit that description. The long haul was only a quarter around the rink before my red light went on. At any early age, maybe six or seven, I had to pull over during an ice-skating race. My competition was gliding forward faster than I could run, and that was exactly what I was doing. Running in my skates, trying my hardest to win. Tears welled up, and it was like my engine was bubbling over. I pulled over and flopped onto a snowbank. My dad came over like a tow truck and rescued me. And the lesson learned was don't run, skate. Even long strokes, combined gliding will be more advantageous. I didn't figure that out until later. It isn't the fast race that I am good at, it's the long haul! What moves me besides my determination are my strong legs. The tortoise and the hare scenario. I'm short, strong-bodied, and determined. Notice I did not say thickheaded, but on occasion, I have been characterized as that as well. Look at the body of the tortoise compared to his head size; it's all determination, nothing else.

I would rather be defeated, knowing that I fully tried, than quit. And if you can laugh at yourself when the chips are down, you are well on your way to survival. Today, if I had to redo that race, I know I would still not win, but at the point of recognizing my inability to surpass my competition, I may have chosen an alternate ending. Engaging in creative skating, turning circles to the fanciest degree I would have known how, and ever so gracefully crossing the finish line perhaps on one leg with the other extended behind me, arms spread out on each side like a small airplane coming in for a landing. At least I would have had the option of completing what I started in a fashion that may have surprised others, but more importantly, provided me with the wisdom that it's ok to finish last, rather than not to have finished at all. Today I take professional skating lessons. And "never give up" is tattooed on my brain. And of course, if someone asked me to help them in a new store adventure, I would probably say yes, but would remember my past experience and the value I have learned to place on myself.

It isn't easy to dust yourself off and try again, but if you have the opportunity, take it. The win isn't the trophy, it's the performance of doing your best until the end.

I was engaged in living my life. From babies, bottles, and the desire to expand my love for art, I was actively pursuing my goals. I raised a family, grew a business, and became involved in my community. I worked out of my home and in plenty of others. Short on a lot of levels, including height, but never on adventure. Keeping the dream to find a store didn't elude me, it only elevated it. Aware that it takes a community to support a small business, I was well on my way. And that's where I knew if there were hurdles in my way, I would jump them. If the sidewalk was icy, I would glide. Each night I would close my eyes and dream of the perfect store, and each day I would search for that store. Van Gogh said, "First I dream and then I paint."

I found the store, and it was perfect for me. I loved the name of the community it was in: Hartland. The street name sounded optimistic as well: Capitol Drive. The brick building was once a car dealership. And ironically, my dad knew of it. It was all meant to be. It was a large storefront with windows for displaying and had a wide sidewalk for pedestrians to walk to and from other small businesses, including restaurants, banks, and a coffee shop called The Pink Mocha. It didn't take long for me to become a frequent consumer of their delicious muffins and sandwiches. The store was 900 square feet, and by taking on the additional back area of 1200 square feet, I had plenty of space. I signed the lease April 1, 2012. It took years for me to acquire this dream, and now I had 21 days to revamp the store and make it my very own. A total makeover: paint, building a cash wrap, granite, lighting, window treatment displays, faux fireplace, restyled kitchen cabinetry, and floor merchandise. A 21-day to-do list for the store to become an extension of everyone's home. Custom artwork, accessories, and design services providing style and distinction.

Wondering if I pulled it off? Yes, I did. After 21 days of hard work and determination, the doors to By Ally's Decorators Warehouse opened on April 21, 2012. And the lesson to this madness is to never give up. See it through to the end. And if I may repeat, yes, *See it through to the end*. April delivered spring excitement, July the summer heat, and September brought in the holidays early – immediately following Halloween décor, Christmas arrived. Whether it was still 85 degrees outside or a day of cool fall air, the temperature inside the store was heating up with its own hustle and bustle. Stockings were being hung by the fireplace, trees sprinkled with twinkling lights, and Bing Crosby played in the background singing "I'll Be Home for Christmas." It was just how I imagined the store to look. Cozy, welcoming, and resembling one's own home. Furniture displayed for gatherings, tables nestled with chairs for conversing, and accessories easily transferable from one room to another. The whole layout of the floor wasn't to "con-flutter." (My word to call out that shopping can be difficult. It can confuse and clutter your mind with complete chaos.) Simplicity is key. To compose the store with an even temperament, a calmness, to allow the shoppers to linger longer, to enjoy the lifestyle I was projecting, even if it were for just a minute or two longer, was my personal goal. Some of my best memories in the store happened around the most magical time of year – Christmas. To those who oppose decorating early, I appreciate your sentiment, and I can see both sides of the season. For myself, commercialism is only subject to the individual whose opinion is just that. For I love this season, and it is far too short no matter how early I start. In September, I start my holiday movies. October, I string my holiday lights. November, I decorate and listen to carols, and by December, I bake cookies and entertain. And somewhere in between, I fit in all the Hallmark movies, ski, catch a snowflake on my tongue, sip coffee in the wee morning, and awe at the snow clinging to the trees. I have always enjoyed late night snowfalls and, after everyone was tucked in, enjoyed walking the streets, making first impressions in the snow. I have discovered most recently that "peace" is what we give ourselves, and we cannot expect others to give it to us.

As 2012 came to an end, and the new year began, so many new avenues were made available for me to explore. I volunteered on the Downtown Business Improvement District Committee and became an Ambassador with the Hartland Chamber of Commerce. Life was good, and my apple cart was just humming along. My kids were great helpers right along with my husband assisting in any way he could. We were a team, and we worked together sometimes just to be together! The calendar months were flying by like in a cartoon, pages torn off like a movie was rolling, and the store was gearing up for its first year. The credits surely noted my family, friends, and clients.

CHAPTER 6

It's Beginning to Rain

It was January 2013, the start of the new year, and second semester. Kevin was a freshman in college and Cal a sophomore in high school. Within a few short months, I'll have been a store owner for one year. How quickly April rolled into May, June, July, and somehow then in October, the clock stopped for a brief second. Out of the blue, Keith announced, "I'm interviewing with so and so next week." My initial reaction was ok, not too alarmed, basically I just tapped the clock, and I was off and running again. I have been known for having selective hearing, and I'm sure my response included, "Ok, great," followed by "Have a nice day, and what time can I expect you home tonight?" Stepping back, I can tell you that I may have been a little too focused on the store. And I am saying that while biting my lip while my eyebrows come together. Keith flew out to California October 3rd for an interview, and though that didn't give me peace, the quietness around the house did. The non-interruptions of my TV shows, and cereal for dinner, or better yet French toast for dinner, was great. The second interview, however, on October 23rd in Houston, threw me for a loop. Now the three H's were upon me. **H**ow the **H**ell did this **H**appen?

It was still just an interview, until it wasn't. And when it became real and he accepted the position, I just went into full denial. Happy for him, but denial that it involved me. In November, Turkey Day preparations stole the show and, of course, letters to Santa followed. As an adult, I still believe in Santa because, the older I get, the more I understand he may need help, so I am the first volunteer. I buy exactly what's on my list and what's on the lists of other family members. As life was getting a little more chaotic at our house and at the store, the snow was also beginning to fly and so were the days. The hold onto your hat scenario, for the wind picked up and temperatures dropped. The frigid air froze moments in time, and one of those moments was the offer letter and Keith's acceptance. I'm sure I "hmmmed." My typical response when I am thinking before speaking. I think I "hmmmed" my way through the entire month of December. Too busy at the store to think, too awestruck at home to respond, I just kept going.

Faster and faster, shoveling the snow, redecorating the store, trimming our family tree, shopping, more decorating, and now airport shuffling. Keith was asked to start December 15th. Briefly looking back, all I can remember was I simplified the equation by thinking he was just going on a vacation and would be back December 24th. So, sending Keith off in December was like the start of another little vacation for myself and Cal. It was a little early Christmas present, and I loved it. I could watch all my Christmas movies for a second time, bake cookies at midnight, jump on the computer at three in the morning, and I could put my pajamas on early, or if I wasn't leaving the house, never change out of them. And for the most part, Cal felt the same way for the first two weeks. This change seemed interesting to both of us. We watched *American Idol* together and bonded. Being a junior in high school really wasn't the year to spend as much time as possible with your mother, but that's what exactly happened. I was the lucky one. When my husband came home for Christmas on the 24th, we celebrated Christmas, enjoyed all our family and friends, and loved the togetherness. The length of his stay turned things back to normal, and the free time allowed us to stay together longer and continue the holiday celebrations.

December 28, 2013 was a turning point for me. The reality of the situation with Keith's new employment was starting to set in. On January 5, 2014, Keith was scheduled to fly back to

California – not just for two more weeks. This time he needed a commitment of moving his family. I knew I was distressed when I decided to get a haircut – and decided to cut it so short that if I put a baseball cap on, any hair left on my head disappeared. It was like a magic trick. The haircut was not a solution and actually created even more stress.

This time around, the departure of all was much more difficult. Kevin returned to college, Keith to California, and Cal back to high school. That left Marlo and me to roam around a very quiet house. I could tell that Marlo felt the loneliness and that too was difficult. She seemed to have aged. Her fur was turning gray, and her eyes seemed very sad. For the first couple of days, I cleaned, organized, did laundry, grocery shopped, and prepared meals. By day four, the house smelled like bleach, the house looked staged, the closets were color organized, and the pantry looked like a photo from a magazine. Back to normal, but empty. My studio received the white glove treatment as well as the store. It was time to SALE out the seasonal and pack away the trees, wreaths, and collection of holiday music. A good friend of mine and her husband assisted in this adventure. Helpful, but looking back now, I think Tim and Cheri came to lighten my spirit, not the actual load of what was being put away. Trying to stay optimistic seemed almost impossible; the fact that I was putting away the holiday décor meant so much more for me this time, for it was going to be the last time I did this at the store. The strategic plan was to operate the store through September of 2014, and then from there, focus on the sale of our family home. I'm not even sure what that meant. In theory, it sounded good, but wait, the only person behind the scenes was me. How do you put a procrastinator in charge of progress on a project that seemed daunting! My personal conviction – I am a procrastinator of things I don't really have an interest in or know how to do! Now with my hair too short, the air too cold, I felt compelled to make decisions that I had control over, and now those were very few and far between. First up, grow my hair out. If I could master that, after having short hair all my life, I could relate to achieving a new personal goal and could reflect on the time it took to move. I think I packed Christmas away for months. At home, the removal of the tree left behind pine potpourri each time I ran the vacuum. And the ornaments were packed this time not just for 11 months of storage, but for taking a trip across country. I was beginning to think of things differently, and shockingly enough to pause and acknowledge that I didn't realize how much time and support my husband had offered me, the kids, the house, and the store. How incredibly supportive and reliable he was. An amazing eye-opener, one that coffee couldn't even match up to. I tried to make up the difference of his hours of contribution and began to use all the hours in my day, and into the next. To combat the extra workload, the process of getting up early and staying up late evolved. Sleep became a luxury, and the routines I had going sustained me through Saturday, but on Sunday I would slow down to the speed of a sloth, not an Ally Cat. What happened after that I cannot explain in detail. I think I was juggling 50 teacups and saucers and wasn't sure if I had time for one more thing, but I tried. I took an evening when Cal had an away game for soccer and decided to have a relaxing massage. It was an hour of pure relaxation. I was putting on my jacket, preparing to walk out of the building, when my phone rang. It was Cal. He needed me to quickly go home and get his jersey that he forgot. All I could think was, *Dang, I want a refund*. Couldn't a massage run like the same program the local car wash had? If it rains within 24 hours, you get to come back for free.

I tried to simplify my life, and the harder I tried, the more complicated it became. I hired a landscaper years ago, and they trimmed my trees to perfection. But the need grew just as the grass did, and I now hired them to cut and edge the lawn. I think they saw me one morning rolling into the subdivision on two wheels just missing their truck, thinking this lady is out of control. Maybe it wasn't my driving, but what I had on when I got out of my car to ask if they could provide service to our address. I had Cal's sweatshirt on, and my pajama bottoms and flip flops in March. I didn't realize it until after I got back in the car. Anyway, they came to my rescue. I enlisted runners to help me, coaxed Kevin to come home on available weekends from college to help, and often bribed kids walking down the sidewalk. In fact, on one evening, the eve before garbage day to be exact, I enlisted Cal's friends to fill any garbage cans in our subdivision that still had available space, for our bins were full. Yes, there is more; I paid someone to take my dog to and from the groomers, hired help to clean my basement storage area, a neighbor to grocery shop, a good friend to shop for clothes for me, and on and on. I personally put on over 25,000 miles a year, so you can only imagine my car's engine and body rarely stopped.

One day, I accepted the invitation to fly out to see Keith and coordinated the coverage at home and at the store. Kevin arranged to drop me off at the airport for a 3:30 p.m. flight. And unfortunately, instead of being prepared, I was running late, and we didn't leave our house until 2:30 p.m. He said he was very disappointed in me. A phrase Keith and I used when our kids were younger as a response to bad choices they may have acted on or referenced. My younger son said to me he would have rather been grounded than hear "I am disappointed." I felt the impact of that, sitting in the passenger seat as my son was driving me to the airport. Thankfully, I made it and boarded the flight for Minnesota with a connecting flight into Orange County. Once in Minnesota, I decided to enjoy lunch. Lunch at Chili's sounded wonderful. A moment to sit back and relax and have a common meal that wasn't so common to me. Taking time for lunch didn't seem like a luxury, but more like a snooze cruise. Lunch interrupted my day, and I would lose all concentration and immediately have an urge to take a nap. So, sleeping on the plane sounded good, and the idea of having lunch on this day could serve me well. I sat down, ordered, and watched the continual hustle and bustle of people coming and going, some with speed and others with the look of determination or exhaustion, I wasn't quite sure. And others, I noticed, had a perplexed look on their face, questioning perhaps where to go next.

My meal arrived in conjunction with the loudspeaker ringing out. I paid more attention to the bleu cheeseburger I just ordered and enjoyed the first bite or two. Then something strange occurred. I wasn't hungry. I was curious more than hungry, and I was beginning to feel uncomfortable. That strange mumbling sound on the loudspeaker was the last boarding call for someone. I glanced at my ticket and immediately saw the boarding time, and an ocean-size wave turned in my stomach. I did not read my ticket correctly. I was supposed to be boarding. By the time I paid my bill and got to the counter, the attendant told me that they had been paging me, and the door on the plane had now been closed and could not be re-opened. Buckets of tears rolled down my face, and soon I was handed the biggest Kleenex box I have ever seen. I told her I would be back once I pulled myself together, and I did.

My first question was, "Are there any flights going back to Milwaukee?" And she replied, "Yes." A yahoo moment, a thrill of excitement, and relief ran through my head, and then I seriously wondered how that would pan out for me? I had to contemplate that scenario for a moment. I would have had to call and arrange for Kevin to pick me up, along with calling Keith to say I wasn't coming. Keith would have understood, Kevin would not have, and I could not hear the disappointment speech twice in one day, so I decided to fly into LAX instead and made the arrangements to do so. This time, I boarded and sat next to a woman and her son. The woman's name was Elsie, and she was saying her rosary, and her son's name was Ralph. They were returning from a family member's funeral. As the plane and passengers were boarding, I noticed the time span was growing, boarding seemed to take forever. And sure enough, an announcement was made that the delay was due to the pilot who was still en route to the airport. My first thought was, *Did he have lunch, followed by a nap, and overslept?*

I called Keith and told him of the second slight delay, and that my battery on my phone was very low, and that I would text him when I landed. All was good, the pilot arrived, the door closed, and we were ready to roll back until we heard the call out that we had to de-ice. The crew circled the aircraft and sprayed the plane's exterior; however, I could smell the fumes through the vents and was beginning to feel sick. The delay required another text message, and now my battery was redlining. I can't even imagine what it was like sitting next to me as I rummaged through my bags, perplexed over the whole trip, exhausted from running late, missing the first plane, and so on. But Ralph, too kind to ask to be moved, reached into his bag and pulled out his "Halo." A mobile charging device for electronics. An incredible lifesaver. How ironic, I have Elsie saying her rosary and Ralph handing me his "Halo." All was going to be ok. I charged both my phone and notebook. And when we finally took off, and beverage service started, I ordered my first cocktail ever on a plane and played Flappy Bird until we landed.

Keith met me at the bottom of the escalator, and as he looked up, I looked down and saw a bouquet of flowers in my path. I think we were both surprised that I made it. I slept the entire car ride back to the apartment.

Southern California in the morning was an eye-opener. The night before, on the plane, it was a lit up like a big game of Lite-Brite, but by the next morning, the land turned into concrete and cars were everywhere. The apartment was right next to the Angels' stadium, and the distance to my husband's work was just a longboarding excursion away. Something he enjoyed, but I never really mastered. Longboarding appeared to be equivalent to my last Razor scooter experience, where the sidewalk abruptly ended and where the grass caught my front tire and Cal's attention as I flipped over the handlebar onto the ground.

But now, our immediate adventure was to find an apartment for Keith until we could join him on the next part of our journey. Bewildered at some of the properties we ran across, I thought it was going to be incredibly difficult to secure a rental unit. And, from my standpoint, the homes we looked at all needed a decorator. A million-dollar house built in the early '80s never had a renovation of any kind. In fact, each chair had the stain from the resting homeowner's head and the carpet was like an airport runway, definitely marked for departures and arrivals and no deviations. What was a heavily traveled path left the outlining carpet looking one inch higher. As we continued our look for an apartment, amenities were a must. We needed a pool, basketball and tennis court, or park nearby. And we needed to hurry up, for my return flight to Wisconsin was within two days. Once we located the unit, I was lucky enough to head back to Wisconsin the following morning, and yes, the return trip was a breeze.

Back in the swing of things, running 100 miles an hour and loving every minute of it, provided the best distraction anyone could ask for.

However, the next trip back to California provided additional obstacles: a plane delay from Milwaukee due to a part needed for the aircraft, a missed connecting flight, and so on. LAX arrivals were becoming very common, and the weather not so. It rained each time I went to visit. The old saying "It never rains in Southern California" is simply not true.

I am notorious for "If it's going to happen, it's going to happen to me." For instance, this episode is a classic. Not pertaining to the move or airplanes, but this moment of truth was on a golf course with my two kids, husband, and dad. We were enjoying a round of golf after completing a motor home excursion to the Black Hills and Mount Rushmore. The trip was also my introduction to wine, which we pulled over for at 10:00 in the morning and started sampling, at least my mom and I did. Two cases later, we were on our way to Menomonie where I had gone to college. Our game of golf was interrupted by a ball heading in our direction. The player called out, and for the most part, we all acknowledged the ball in course, and honestly without my glasses on, I thought it was coming straight for me. I started taking a couple quick steps back and tripped over Keith's golf bag, and splat. An eagle referenced in the game of golf became a spread eagle for me on the ground. Dazed and confused at the new level I was playing at, I couldn't stop laughing, nor could my family surrounding me.

This type of experience was not uncommon for me. The ski trip in high school put me on the top of the largest hill, and when I went to clean my glasses, they snapped in half. Playing basketball, balls in the air remarkably bopped me in the head. So, as the saying goes, "When you are given lemons, make lemonade." Does that also apply to six-hour layovers in Denver, CO? My husband was notorious for booking flights that encountered unexpected delays. But in Denver, where there's smoke, start smoking? Or was that just smoke coming out of my ears when the layovers were six hours and counting?

When Keith would call or text or even email, he would say he was "living the dream." "Seventy-five degrees and sunny every day." In return, I would turn up the thermostat to 75 and agree. However, I was living a nightmare, not a dream. As February ended and we marched into the next month, the concept of moving was really beginning to sink in. The ice was melting, and my brain was finally comprehending the onset of change that was occurring. All the twinkling lights had been packed away, and now the only distraction was the list of to-do items that outran my average two-page list and turned it into five.

Spring came, and the onset of what to do with the store ran through my head. If you were wondering why this book takes you through the history of becoming a small business owner, then your answers will be met in this chapter. Leaving my store was not an option. I didn't want to close or say "moving" or even acknowledge that the store could be anything other than a design store. The emphasis on finding someone who loved decorating was my goal. The store was a dream I had just made into a reality, and I wasn't ready for it to be over. This one challenge challenged me beyond all others. Quitting was not an option, nor was flopping into a snowbank. I worked too hard and long at finding the store, and I knew I would do just the same finding someone who could take it over. I networked. I asked. I inquired. I became an agent even before I became a licensed real estate agent for that matter. It truly was not my responsibility to find a tenant, yet when others heard of my intent, they questioned my motives. I didn't have a responsibility, I had the ability. My heart called me to the task. I couldn't let my dream fade away, and to keep it alive, I had to find another passionate soul. I remember gathering at a local restaurant in our small town for a Chamber Ambassadors meeting. And here is where my title of Ambassador hit the pavement. I acted on the behalf of myself, the small business owner, trying to keep and attract small businesses to the community. I shared my goal with my fellow members, and it proved to be the winning choice. One of the members, an insurance agent, referred me to a client who was looking for a storefront. This person's name was so familiar, and it just so happened they came into the store and sold me pillows early on. The connection was immediate, and an affirmation of what a Chamber does was validated right in front of me.

I called her in early July, and she was eager to meet and as enthusiastic as I was. She said yes to the store, and the landlord said yes as well. By the time September rolled around, my days were counting down as hers were gearing up. My last day at the store seemed like a daydream. It was September 30, 2014. I didn't have any control over the time, or the ability to covet one second. The day was dedicated to inventory, with the assistance of two friends Diane and Wayne, and the evening to gathering my personal things. I didn't have time to dwell on my departure, toast a glass of champagne, or shed a tear. The clock somehow knew that the moments needed to be filled with movement for me to say "Goodbye."

At 9:00 p.m. that evening, Cal confided in me that he wasn't feeling well, and before I knew it, I was driving him to the emergency room. And at that same moment, my heartache for the store turned into my concern and love for my child, and that the greater reason for "being" prevailed – being MOM to my kids was and is my greatest achievement. After 11:00 p.m. that evening, we left the emergency room together with good news and went home.

Everything I mentioned earlier that seemed important to me came down to one thing. And the incredible lists of things I still needed to do or wanted to do at the store vanished into thin air. The realization that I was not in control miraculously made its appearance at the right time, at the right moment, and for the right reason. And all the planning and list-making and good intentions could not prevail over the true priority in my life. By the next morning, I realized I didn't have a to-do list – I had a "to-love list." And the only thing on it was taking care of my family.

With a new owner at the store, my home studio once again became my workplace, and my gal pal Marlo loved it. She followed me around the house and would often lie on the floor next to me as I sewed or painted in my studio. Her company kept me calm, and my company gave her comfort. At 11 years old, far beyond the hot dog days, or pounds of turkey, she needed comfort and companionship. I often reflect on the day we added her to our family, and often think that she too was adopting us. I guess her running makes me wonder if I too was running too fast back then? By now, however, we were in routines that provided us so much joy. In the evening, around the same time every night, Marlo would jump on the bed and would warm up my side. And in return, each evening I would take off my warm bathrobe and lay it on the carpet for her to lie on. This routine was only modified if Cal wasn't home yet, for then she would hop off my bed and lie at the bottom of the stairs until he came home. Once he was in his bed, she would climb the stairs, and you could hear her charms softly ringing. Each night, this routine gave my son and me comfort. In the morning, she would either be down at the bottom of the stairs waiting for us, or on the sofa, perched to look out the window. She greeted everyone who came to the door, and all were welcomed. Her Airedale manner was just that playful.

The kids taught her how to play soccer, and I think she preferred that over swimming. Perhaps she didn't like getting her soft curls wet. Marlo preferred to ride in the front seat regardless if there was a passenger already there. She was my big lap dog. Seventy-eight miles one way to Chilton may have been a discomfort, but I loved it. When she was a puppy, I rode with her on my lap, and it connected me to how she was feeling. She was carsick until the age of two, and when I was feeling a little woozy, I knew she was also, and I would pull over for her.

She loved opening presents, to the point that when we tried rewrapping one, she gave us a very disappointed look. She was our brown-eyed, brunette girl. Loveable and loyal to whoever loved her up. Perhaps sneaking her out of her kennel at night after the boys went to bed was the reason she really became my girl. Or was it the mornings after I would prepare breakfast for the boys and then sit on the kitchen floor with my back to the refrigerator and hand-feed her. Whatever the reason, she was adorable. Named after Marlo Thomas, "That Girl," she was my girl. She grew up to be quite the photogenic dog, and her pictures tell a story of their own. She enjoyed having her family close, and that meant all of us.

The transition was difficult for her as well. The month of October, after I relinquished the store, she remained by my side. In evenings, she would first lie next to the fireplace, and then make her way to the sunroom to enjoy the cool air. It was Saturday, October 28th. Cal and I took her to the farmers market in the morning. In the late afternoon, she stayed with Cal when I ran to see a client. By 8:00 that evening, we were making our way to the ER vet. My son drove our red Suburban, and just like when she was a puppy, she rode on his lap. Marlo didn't come home with us that night. She went to her new home, Heaven. Pause is the only word that resembles that evening. One heart stopped beating, and two others broke. Tears poured over her as we sat on the cold floor and nestled her in my son's sweatshirt. Life had suddenly taken an unexpected turn, and the pain of grief, disbelief, and loneliness crept into the room and went home with us.

My son called his friend to join him that evening, and they left together. I left the parking lot and pulled out within a foot or two of striking a truck heading west. It was that moment when your heart falls below your feet that you must pull yourself together and refocus not only on the road you are on, but on the path you are traveling. Prayers guided me home that evening, for I knew I wasn't driving alone. For that matter, I wasn't prepared to hear that Marlo had unannounced tumors surrounding her vital organs and was bleeding internally. Her passing relieved her pain, and it pronounced ours. And now, perhaps you may think that it was our nightly routine that was so engrained in us, but for three evenings after her passing, I could hear Marlo's soft jingling of her charms that she wore around her neck softly announcing that she was coming up the stairs. I believe it was her announcement letting us know she was ok. She is forever with us.

The timing of everything seemed so surreal. The store's transition gave me real time with my Marlo, and for that I am forever "great-full." And to the woman who first sold me pillows and then came back into my life for a reason, beyond reasons I have endless gratitude. The store is still operating today and is beautiful. Nestled in the little downtown area that is steadily expanding, yet so quaint. It's an attraction all its own, and it pulls you in to a time of community. It's all that and more. It's the store that put my life into perspective and rewarded me with an achievement of inner personal success. I didn't give up on a dream or on myself.

CHAPTER 7

For Sale by Owner

Days of the hustle and bustle were now slowing down, even though the holidays were gearing up. It was November 2014, then December, and then I turned 50. What the heck? I don't want to turn 50, or move at the age of 50 for that matter. I have been in the same state since I can remember. Born in Illinois, yes, but that doesn't count. And moving forward now just seemed like moving all uphill as I was about to be heading downhill. And guess what? I was tired. I pushed myself to the point of exhaustion. Keith surprised me with a 50th birthday vacation to Dana Point, CA, and for the first two days, I slept. It was much-needed rest so I could make it through the next big hoop, which was selling our home in Wisconsin. If we sold too early, we would need somewhere else to live. And if we didn't sell in time, then what? This was Cal's last semester as a senior, and preparation of what lay ahead was foreign to the both of us. January rolled into February, and February rolled into me taking a faux painting job for a client whose husband once employed mine, 23 years ago. And 23 years ago, it started off like this: One Sunday morning after a routine walk to a local convenience store to get two muffins, two coffees, and one Sunday paper, my goal was to look for a new position for my husband. Our apartment, brand-new when we moved in, served us well, but with Kevin being born, my instinct was to move into a home and settle into a neighborhood with lots of kids. So, in order to move the train down the track and get set, it was time for a new career, and literally, there it was in black and white: Manufacturing Supervisor. Keith forwarded his resume and was hired. Years later, he decided to move on to another company and did so, but I remained in contact with his previous employer and was often hired for my artistic work. From faux painting, to constructing and fabricating headboards, to other upholstery work, I continued with that relationship that today has come full circle. I shared with my client that we were moving to California, and as bizarre as it sounded to me to hear myself say it, I think it sounded more bizarre to her. I couldn't believe the words that were coming out of my mouth, and I don't think she did either. It had to be the paint fumes getting to me, or was I coming down with something? Seriously, at that very moment, I felt like I was telling a lie. I didn't believe it, how could anyone else?

My client—wife, mother of two, intuitively wise, and degreed in law—immediately began asking me questions. She asked about my younger son, and would he be moving with us? And our older son, would he be joining us after he finished college? I think the more questions she asked, the faster I painted. And I'm sure the look on my face was that of bewilderment. I don't think I was ever asked or immediately answered all those questions at one time. It was like a cartoon moment with captions popping out of my head filled with question marks and the realization that I didn't know what to plan for or what was happening. My client then said she had a lake house we could rent if we needed a temporary place to live. And the next time my husband flew home, we were invited to stop out and look at it, and we did.

She also offered the contact information of a friend of hers who was in the real estate business if I decided to go with a realtor. Her company had been the largest real estate company in the state of Wisconsin since 1946. My client said she would have her friend call me, and immediately, the agent did. I agreed to have her meet me at our house and she sat down with me at our kitchen table and reviewed what her company had to offer. I already felt in charge of everything and couldn't let go of anything. After she left, I knew I was going to be a maverick. I just felt it in my bones that I was going to do it my way, no matter what, a classic character reference of me, I guess. The agent presented her materials, and to my embarrassment, I didn't pay attention. Her real estate knowledge surpassed mine, and if I would have taken the time to understand the process, the process wouldn't have put 25 new things on my list but would have added to hers. I didn't want to sell, and I was restless; I couldn't calm my nerves long enough to read the materials after she left. But what was left now was little time for me to get the house on the market and sold, so I began to question: For sale by owner? For sale by a firm? Not for sale? Never for sale? Hmmm, I had to think about that. I started with never for sale, let's keep it. My husband told me then to go online and look at homes in Southern California. Dealing with reason, I was left with let's rent it out. The next response was, if you don't mind renting to potential strangers and incurring repair costs and possible damage to your property, then ok, let's think about renting. And that turned the thought back to selling. And with family in the business, how about putting a family real estate sign in our yard? Much to my surprise, my dad said I could sell the house on my own, and he would assist if needed. With over 40 years of real estate experience, his confidence in me along with my knowledge of the home seemed to be the right choice. Hello Kinko's, I need a sign! A week later, Cal put the sign in the front yard, and I put it on

Zillow. The memory of the sign going in the yard was captured with a photo. Symbolic of strength and forward thinking.

The first offer we received and accepted had a home sale contingency. Clueless to what that meant at the time, I was excited and thrilled that we sold our home. It was weeks later, however, that the contingencies were not met, and the offer fell apart. I was also told by a close relative that an accepted offer does not mean it's sold. A few days later, we received another offer above asking price and closed on the sale of our home. The family who purchased our home are now our friends. The direct connection of providing for their family aided us in providing for ours. And the connection of staying in contact with my husband's previous employer provided a lake home for our family, and all seemed right with the world. The countdown of days until Cal completed his senior year were dialing down into the single digits, and yes, my hair was growing out. The year and a half of living apart was now beginning to come to an end.

We moved into the lake house on May 12th, and our first night, as we rolled down the big hill toward the house and lake, it was pitch-black. It had to have been close to 9:00 p.m., and both my kids were with me. As we started walking towards the house, a voice called out. "Hey, what are you doing? Are you the folks from Pewaukee?" The man started making his way towards us, and coming from a subdivision full of streetlights, we were now left in the dark and not quite sure what to expect. He introduced himself as he came closer for us to see his face and welcomed us. His name was Mark, a neighbor from on the top of the hill. I can't remember exactly what my youngest son said after he walked away, but it resembled something like this: "He came down to introduce himself because he is going to kill us tonight in our sleep." Happy thoughts and lots of prayers were said together that evening. Case in point, if you are going to move into a house at night in pure darkness, amid unfamiliar territory, wait until morning. But we were beyond that and were trying just to get inside. Once inside, we immediately locked the doors and laughed, and yet that first night, I think we all slept with one eye open. By next morning, we were all a little tired, but pros on handling our first move.

Cal finished high school, and we celebrated with a party. That same week, I drove to Madison and met my husband's boss, Claude, and his wife, Ruth. Hopeful that Ruth and I could become friends, I proceeded with optimism. We both sat through a presentation or two with our husbands and then excused ourselves to walk the Square and window-shop together. Within a little time, the path that we were on took us by shops that we shared similar interests in. Our conversation grew with each step around the block and included our families, our kids, art, cooking, and more. *Incredible*, I thought. *This is going to be a blast!* I'm meeting a new friend in Wisconsin and soon we will be friends in California. By the end of the week, Keith flew back to California, and the next time we were going to see each other, we would be driving to California together to meet up with Cal, who was already in California vacationing with his friends. A graduation gift, or Mom's way of nurturing the move from one state to another while still being surrounded by familiarity, his best buds. Let me just say, it worked out for him. As for myself, this is where the road ends and the storms create a landslide – it heads south from here!

CHAPTER 8

How to Live in the Wild Wild West

Moving to California was not an act of nature, though something did move my feet. Keith was offered an opportunity of a lifetime, and the opportunity for him manifested into a stark realization for me. Keith appreciated being recognized and sought after by a world-renowned leader in oil. Instead of embracing a move from Wisconsin to California, I sheepishly found myself admitting that I selfishly replaced *we* with *me* years ago, and I didn't want to move.

Nevertheless, my husband's face revealed happiness, and for the first time in a long time, I saw it. It was a revelation, and the earth shook like a sand globe. All of California may have felt the aftershock, but only one house, with one real estate sign, in one small community was affected. My contention, where the sand fell, it fell from the hands of people, not nature. Intentionally placed, ever so mindfully, on the house that we bought.

I believe the plot of this story was concocted months before our initial move, and the casting call was a real estate sign purposely placed in the ground with the intent to deceive. Luring us in where the stage had been set, and where the sand intentionally lay, disguising the place we soon called home. And now, as the new homeowner, in a new state, each layer of sand brushed aside produced a chilling, jaw-dropping, eye-widening realization, followed by greater uncertainty. I truly felt like I was in the sand globe, hands up to the glass pounding for help. But like a real estate sign that disappears after a sale, so did the agents and their firms.

Yes, our new home was the cause of a lot of apprehension, followed by months of sleepless nights. I took off my rose-colored glasses and started keeping an eye on what I felt was keeping an eye on me. Yes, the twists and turns of moving from Wisconsin to California and back again within two years, accompanied by the real estate contracts produced along the way, changed more than my physical address today, it changed my life forever. This story is far greater than any reality TV series or HGTV show imaginable, and somehow, I misconstrued Homes for Holmes, and that's Sherlock Holmes by the way, and went from decorator to investigator overnight.

For creative as I thought I was, and, with a little kindness to myself, may still be, my home décor story takes a twist far off the foreseeable trail of just moving across country. Dreaming of a new area to live, along with a new house to decorate, was going to be an adventure. At least that's how I sold myself on moving. But, somehow, West took me too far left and left me too far wrong! If that's not already a cliché, it should be. Right with life is where I wanted to move, but left with bewilderment started rolling in the further we drove away from my familiar surroundings: Wisconsin.

The Wisconsin to California departure date, planned two years, four months, and three days in advance, still came as a surprise to me the day it finally arrived. It was the day of all days, and when I should have been ready, I clearly wasn't. And, like an alarm clock, I hit the snooze button indefinitely. I dug my heels into my beloved state of Wisconsin, and our scheduled Friday 9:00 a.m. departure time turned into a 7:30 p.m. circus. I visited four clients, tacked up a bed skirt, returned an airport rental car, and stopped in Whitewater for a brief visit to give my older son Kevin a haircut. The ultimate phrase I used on my kids when they were growing up was "Just about." "Mom, are you ready?" "Just about." "Is dinner ready?" "Just about." And, "Are you almost done cutting my hair?" "Yep, just about." And now for myself, my son's hair couldn't get any shorter, and I was all out of time and excuses. The electric razor was unplugged, the maroon cape was unsnapped, and the neck was dusted off. This chapter of cutting my kid's hair had just ended, and the tools were tossed into the green dumpster next to the house that my son would be calling his Wisconsin home. The era of "just about" just ended.

We now entered the "now" phase. At 7:30 p.m., the closing of two car doors and the start of the ignition brought the end and the beginning simultaneously together. As we slowly drove out of the gravel parking lot with the windows down, waving goodbye, I had a crushing feeling, matching the sound of the tires rolling over the gravel. And as we prepared to turn right, we pacified our minds by looking forward to meeting up with Cal, who just graduated from high school and was vacationing with his friends in sunny California. A week at our time-share and a day or two at our new apartment was a prelude to what life would be like for Cal beginning a new life in a new state. The best part, however, was that he was surrounded by his best buds.

With an overpacked Suburban (capacity of eight) we departed with barely room for two. Despite the overpowered engine and the excitement of the driver, the weather forecast within the cabin was emotionally cloudy with a 100 percent chance of precipitation. A storm was brewing. My tears started rolling as we rolled out of Wisconsin, and for the most part, I wasn't asked to drive. My glasses didn't have wipers, and I think Keith feared that if he had fallen asleep, I would have turned the Suburban around and headed back to Wisconsin. I married a wise man.

The first hour driving seemed surreal. The sun was setting as we departed, and we merely drove to Iowa our first night. Not bad, not bad at all. I still had a chance to call a cab or my dad. The next day, however, we drove, argued, and somehow ended up having to backtrack 20 miles into Denver to stay at the Downtown Marriott. Downtown Denver provided a diversion for the night. As we pulled up to valet parking, nothing was left to the empirical fact that we were moving. Bikes on the back and car packed floor to ceiling left very little room for me to change my mind. The cargo area shifted during transit, and what seemed to have been packed with assemblance just melted into one big pile. My makeup and quick toiletries for instance were in an open tray, not a traveling case. And each time my husband opened the back after taking the bikes off, the caddy fell to the ground and dispersed everywhere. I collected the contents, grabbed the container, and proceeded to walk into the lobby of the hotel. It didn't take long to notice I was extremely misplaced. I was amazed at the event currently happening. From evening attire to floor-length gowns, my yoga pants and t-shirt didn't quite fit the bill. A quick check-in and nod towards the elevators was all I needed.

Ironically, I noticed directly across the street was the

Denver courthouse, and much to my disappointment, it was closed – for my first order of business that morning would have been divorce court! In all fairness, I didn't plan one single thing on this trip out, and because of that, I should not have complained, but I did. The next morning, I reluctantly got back into the Suburban on the passenger side, and we drove in silence until we saw the sunlight hitting the mountains. And with this beautiful display of God's craftsmanship, I was called back to reality and the thought that with faith, the move was for a reason. So onward we traveled. Of course, I was still not sharing in the driving, for in my husband's eyes, I was still a flight risk. The majestic mountains calmed my wild spirit, and I think we enjoyed each other's company from that moment on. And soon, yes, I was asked to drive.

I was inspired by a motor home that was ahead of us, carrying kids' bikes on the back end, cruising at speeds well above 80. The driver's maneuvering skills were amazing. The road was their raceway. And the ability to come up with a story behind the fast-moving RV was mine: She left him behind? She's driving and he's sleeping? They just left the kids at Grandma's house? My sense of humor was finally catching up. I tried Facebooking the whole time, but the mountains made it difficult. Boredom set in as we entered Utah. I should have flown. I personally would have had more leg room, a tray to hold my drink and the opportunity to have an empty seat next to me to sprawl out. Flying also would have equated to a vacation perhaps, and not a permanent move. Driving literally and visually put distance between what I was accustomed to and new and unfamiliar territory.

Yet, three days later, we arrived at the perfect place for this story to begin, classic California. The land where stories evolve, movies are filmed, and anyone who is a character can blend in.

If you recall, I labeled myself as an artistic character and never truly adapted to the interior design label, or decorator, but stepped out as a Home Décor Artist. Yes, I see myself as being very creative, and as one client put it, "unique." I have mixed paints, mixed textures, created and re-created artwork, built furniture, and laddered walls exceeding 21 feet. But never in my wildest imagination could I ever have fabricated a story such as this even if I used all my creativity at once! "How the West Was Won" is not a chapter in this book, but "How to Live in the Wild Wild West" is! My story unloads, unpacks, and undeniably over-delivers on the encounters that took place which evolved into the chapters you are about to read. You may find all 29 of them to be fictional, but I find them therapeutic, especially Chapter 24.

Quick insight, if you are thinking of moving to California, prepare to rewrite your list of items to bring, and include, from my personal experience, the following: You are going to need more than a Wisconsin driver's license to get your California license, and be sure to bring your passport, for you will definitely feel like you are entering a foreign country. You will also need a detective license, DNA test strips, video camera, tape recorder, camera with professional zoom lens, computer, cell phone, patience, law degree, a Smith & Wesson, and of course, a trail of gluten-free breadcrumbs to find your way back to your home state. And if I may add one additional crucial element, bring God along. God will not need a forwarding address, but constant communication is advisable. Also, just to be safe, get yourself a real estate license if you plan on purchasing, renting, or just looking at real estate. One would think Hollywood actors and actresses would only prevail in Hollywood, that a movie script or book so preposterous as this would only come from a film director. Perhaps the heat has taken its toll on many of my California acquaintances, along with droughts, fires, and earthquakes, but somewhere along the way, the whole state has become a mirage. Or perhaps the thesaurus version of mirage; "fake" would have been a better word choice.

No earthquakes noted on our way into the state, just a little turbulence within the cabin caused by the continual storms of emotions. And with that being said, my normal verbal expression of "Holy buckets" graduated to "What the heck!?"

Entering California was uneventful, and brown. The drought took its toll on the countryside and the lush green grasses were replaced with tumbleweeds and a yellow haze that hung over the mountains. The heat was intense; temperatures were in the hundreds. East of the ocean and west of the mountains, we finally parked the Suburban under an awning, numbered and assigned to us. Anaheim Hills became our next temporary home where we started the next phase of our lives. We met up with Cal, who was already at the apartment, and then the moment of truth came; this is home! Not so sure if I wanted to unpack the Suburban or head back, I decided to take a nap. I remember closing my eyes and trying to decipher if it was motion sickness from the long-ass car ride or if it was the heat already getting the best of me. I truly believed the best of me was left 2,000 miles away.

CHAPTER 9

Instant Replay

As captured earlier on the radar screen, the drive to California had a forecast of precipitation, and believe me, it rained inside the cabin. If someone followed me around the morning we were supposed to leave at 9:00 a.m., they would have found Velcro on the bottom of my shoes. I was sticking to the fact that I didn't want to leave the state, but now that we'd arrived, I was truly in a state of disbelief.

Not too long after I closed my eyes, I awoke in the same place. I wasn't dreaming. This was really happening. And the request of "Let's go the beach" put me right back into the Suburban. The beach was only 20 minutes away, with six lanes in each direction and cars traveling at incredible speeds. It was only going to take us about an hour and a half with some slowdowns and complete stops to get there, and so it began.

The sun was extremely intense, and the sand even hotter. I managed to skip and hop my way to the blanket and lounge chair. Sitting idle, and now coastal, was a miracle. Our first day in California, and we were already at the beach. The spot we selected immediately drew the Pacific Coast guard vehicle to park right behind me. Perhaps it was the white glow my body gave off, or the need for more than SPF 50. Whatever the case, I felt assured, in case of a spontaneous explosion, that I was in good hands. The temperatures never dropped below 80, and oftentimes climbed into the 100's and even creeped up to 114. My summer wardrobe from Wisconsin consisted of capris, flip flops, lightweight sweaters, and mosquito spray. However, things were about to get real here. I needed flip flops exclusively, sunscreen, and a hat with a large brim to cover my shoulders. Counting the number of redheads on the beach was quite entertaining. We came and left with the same number.

The apartment was air-conditioned, but three people in a studio was hot no matter what the real temperature was. I wanted to go back to Wisconsin, Cal never wanted to come out, and Keith was the referee and often the "fall guy" for the blame, boredom, and anxiousness we all shared. The plague of boredom for my son kept me very busy. Normally, the summer after graduation and before college, kids would work and gather nightly to do whatever kids do. But this was not the case. For the most part, Cal and I entertained each other, and we looked forward to Dad returning from work so he could entertain us for the rest of the evening. I think we waited all day for him to come home. And with this as our expectation, our routines fell quickly into place. Keith went to work, I watched the clock, and Cal stayed glued to his phone. For myself, I was hopeful my phone would ring. So many people told us that they would show us the area. The insurance company we switched everything to, the mortgage company we aligned with, the relocation company, our real estate agent, friends from my husband's work, and so on, but this was not the case. If you recall, prior to our late June departure from Wisconsin, I was able to meet Ruth in Madison, WI. I felt as though everything would come together. But by the time we arrived and settled into our apartment, the concerning fact for me was, no one called, and I was missing pieces to this move. I didn't need a red carpet rolled out, but an extension of hospitality would have been well-received. What I did receive was an invitation to a baby shower in honor of Ruth's daughter-in-law, and I joyfully accepted. I had never met the momma-to-be, but I was going to. By this time, I would have done anything to have met other women.

Happier days were on the horizon. I shopped for a gift, put a dress on, and drove myself to the party. Huge accomplishment for me – it was my first road trip on my own into the city. Glasses, check. Gas, check. Cell phone charger, check. Confidence, check. On time? No. First clue to myself, I was nervous. Sweaty palms and white knuckles all the way into Orange. I was greeted by Claude's sister, who introduced herself as Gayle, the artist. Gayle then directed me to Ruth. Immediately, I could see how well-bonded this family was and what an opportunity it was going to be to spend the afternoon with them. I was seated at the family table, however, Ruth acknowledged she would be far too busy to sit with me, but kindly introduced me to her family who was already seated. I immediately sat between two women. The woman to my right was Claude's sister-in-law, Ramona, and to my left was Richard's wife, Patsy. Richard would soon be known as Dick, our realtor. Directly across from me was the matriarch of the family, and left and right of her, her two daughters, Gayle and Mabel. I remember being offered sunscreen and asked if I wanted to be seated in the shade. Was it the glare I gave off with my light-colored dress and matching skin tone? I was just in awe of the planning that had to have taken place for this baby shower event. The backyard was decorated beautifully. The incredible array of themed décor, from the trees, to table settings, to party favors, made this baby shower seem somewhat magical. It was Disney in the backyard. Everything looked perfect, including Ramona's hair, so I complimented her. I also asked for her hairdresser's name or number, and she replied with, "I have been going to her for over 20 years, but I can't recall her number or name of her salon." She then got up from the table and walked away. Hmmm . . . was it something I said?

Next, I was approached by Mabel, whose daughter was Patsy, married to our soon-to-be agent, to see if I would like a tour of the pottery studio that her sister Gayle works out of. Immediately, my spirits were rekindled. All was not lost. I enjoyed my time, and as I drove back to the apartment, I was finally able to exhale. In fact, a day or two later, I sent a thank-you text to Ruth for the shower invitation and expressed my gratitude for being invited. I also returned an invitation if she would be so interested to spend a week with me in Wisconsin in September. If I couldn't trust my husband's boss's wife, who could I trust?

With this being said, I think I just slipped into the California abyss and "What the frock!?" evolved. Not a pleasant word choice by any means, but definitely shared by Kate with her question back to me, "You invited a complete stranger to spend a week with you in Wisconsin? WTF?"

Swearing has never been a good look for me. Something about it sounds absolutely uneducated. But for the most part, when used in conversations between family members, especially when on the phone, make me laugh, and laugh hard. A twisted sense of humor perhaps, but when swearing, I can feel the stress dissolve quickly. It has been known and shared by others that swearing has a physical impact, making one stronger, less stressed, and more resilient.

By laughing, I embraced my sense of humor and medicated my woes. And by now, each routine 7 a.m. phone call to my sister, Kate, amongst 20 or more throughout the day, was comforting. Sometimes all you need is for someone to pick up the phone, and it can lead to someone picking up your spirits and lightening your load even when you're thousands of miles apart.

Raised Catholic, parochial-schooled, and somewhat even-tempered, using four-letter words was seldom, like holidays, or saved for special occasions. From my mouth to listening ears, even from across the phone lines, I could see eyebrows raise and jaws drop. If my dad picked up the phone, his seriousness usually diffused the conversation, and within a short span, he handed the phone over to my mother – a classic maneuver within our household. And once she got on the phone, the first words that came out of her mouth were, "Hello, Ally, what's up?" Was it the facial expression Dad made while handing over the phone or was it the volume at which I spoke and the speed at which the words rolled off my tongue that was alarming? Or was it my final WTF?

Whatever the scenario, it worked. My mom, now on the other end of the receiver, refocused my energy and mindset back on my family and picked me up as she has done throughout my life. In a recent conversation, she pointed out that for the first nine months, it was just the "two of us." However, when I entered the world, I was graced with three immediate siblings and was followed by two more. This made dialing a sibling quite easy and left no one off the hook if one of us had an emergency. What a sweetheart, with six kids and only two ears, the stories she's heard could fill a library.

The act of handing over the phone to my mom was brilliant, and it allowed for my voice to drop an octave. She would put the phone back to my dad's ear for encouraging words. Never to further ignite the situation, but to diffuse it, without completely snuffing out the fire. Insisting never to quit but to get back up on the horse. And how appropriate to reference a horse, for this story takes place in Norco, California, Horsetown, USA. A place where I completely fell off the horse and landed in a pile of $h?t, figuratively speaking.

By now, my daily routine resulted in wake up, play tennis, shower, play tennis, shower, play tennis, sit by the pool, play tennis, shower. A week into this routine, we needed a boost and added a couple of TV shows: *The Office* and *Modern Family*. *The Office* was also enjoyed by the tenant upstairs. He watched *The Office* all night long and into the early mornings, and the theme song which introduced and concluded each episode kept my son and I awake. Of course, we had a lumberjack/baritone player sawing wood all night as well. Each night, the race was on in the apartment as to who was going to fall asleep the fastest. Well, I can assure you it wasn't me, and often, it wasn't my son either. It was the noisemaker, who could hit the pillow and immediately snore through the night. By week three, I was already sleep-deprived and climbing the walls. I just ran a marathon preparing for this big move, and somehow I ended up in a tiny, tiny apartment wondering how to fill my days.

Plain as day, and as bored as I ever thought possible, I finally hit a brick wall. So busy one day and nothing at all to do the next left me perplexed and in a state of confusion. I needed a new remedy and pulled out my sewing machine, and it was a cause for my son and I to look for a fabric store. Cal was happy I found something to pacify my time, and I was happy I made him drive us around to explore new areas.

Yes, I packed my sewing machine in our Suburban. The prolonged departure before we left Wisconsin was full of sewing and tacking up the bed skirt, if you recall. But what I failed to pack was everything else I had mentioned earlier, including the magnifying glass and binoculars and so on.

Here in our little apartment, I started sewing again. I made a little purse to carry my cell phone, driver's license, and debit card. The "bare" necessities needed to escape the bear state.

CHAPTER 10

House Hunting without a Gun

Locked and loaded, we were back into the Suburban within a week of our arrival to start our first day of house hunting. Driving through a quaint area close to one of my husband's co-workers, we noticed several homes for sale and pulled the trigger on one by calling the number on the sign. We reached the owner/contractor of the property, and the message was live. He didn't have time to meet us, and reasonably so, for it was July 3rd, a holiday weekend, but he did offer the lockbox code and told us to look at it on our own. I was definitely surprised that this was how they did things in California. Incredible, this wasn't going to be as bad as I believed it to be. People here must be trustworthy . . . Wow, we were onto something remarkable and somewhat familiar. A white fence enclosed this yellow ranch home on a quiet street, not far from shopping, coffee shops, and a small main street of activity. We unlocked the house, entered, and were surprised to see what a $600,000 house offered. Amid slanting floors, small rooms, and a tiny kitchen, there was a pool immediately off the kitchen patio doors. Just the thought of being able to get a house with a pool kept us intrigued as we closed and locked the door on this house and became more intrigued house hunting for others. Maybe house hunting wasn't going to be so bad. I'm sure many of you are probably thinking, "Why the rush?" Why not live in an area and rent, then buy later? Well, just for the record, we are now trying to cohabitate after living separately for the past year and a half, in a small shoebox, in a new state, without any belongings that resemble home, with one of our sons and not the other, without my store, while being lulled nightly to sleep, or not, by our baritone/lumberjack. My vote was to buy a house. My husband's boss, Claude, also said we should commit and buy a house. Perhaps it was twofold; commit and buy a house and use my nephew Dick as your real estate agent. Whatever the case, we continued to search for homes on our own as well and called on our next property to see. This time, we stopped at a home with a sign in the front yard, knocked on the front door, and were greeted by the owners. The owners asked us to follow real estate protocol and contact the listing agent first. So, we called the listing agent, and when we asked to see the home, she said, "If you're already there at the house, the homeowners can take you through." Interestingly enough, they did, and it encouraged a second showing.

Unfortunately, the second time we went through the house, with the listing agent and my husband's co-worker, what we saw were not opportunities, but deterrents to the home. We had too many concerns, and the fact that it was surrounded by rental properties did not suit us well. With the advice provided, and well-taken, we departed and were thankful for the opportunity. Continuing our search, we drove our three-mile radius around our apartment and soon extended it to five and six miles, then 12 and 15 miles. The days seemed like weeks, and without anything else to do, house hunting was our focus.

Finally, out of despair, we took Claude's suggestion and called upon his nephew, Dick, to be our real estate agent. We looked high and low, at prices as well as location. Mountains or ocean or somewhere in between. I referenced earlier the homes which looked like they were built in the '80s but not updated since. This seemed to be the general scenario. The older the home, the more work each seemed to need. It was a complete mystery to me as to how fancy cars and showy houses on the outside didn't replicate what was happening on the inside. Our prior searches on our own ended each weekend with disappointment, and our agent was truly needed. We originally thought if we found a home of interest, he could take us through. But there had to have been a better plan, and there was.

Yes, I could have gone with my sister Kate, who has been a licensed broker for the past 28 years in Northern California, but she mentioned something like Northern California and Southern California are not the same. And from what I could already tell, she was right.

With little experience in home buying, we were going to rely on the nephew. The one and only home we purchased in Wisconsin was from a reputable builder. A brand-new home, complete with building permits, blueprints, inspection signoffs, and the benefit of no previous homeowner history. Prior to that, we lived in a new apartment. New appliances, carpet, furnace, and AC, and again, no previous tenant. By far, this made looking for a new home that much more difficult. Once having my family close to now leaving everything behind left me with higher expectations, resulting in greater disappointment. Something greener must be on the other side, right? We are in sunny California, where the sun shines brightly and there is enough vitamin D for everyone to be happy.

CHAPTER 11

Re-loading

Each weekend, we packed into the Suburban and headed out to see open houses posted on Zillow, Trulia, and an array of other sites. We also drove around neighborhoods aimlessly, hopeful for a for sale sign or an open house sign directing us to tour the home. We viewed one home that Dick recommended; however, without having any idea of what we were looking for, the house did not fit our criteria, but the experience was educational. It's far easier to define what you do not like, prompting cues to search for the opposite. Land was a factor, limited in some areas, and sometimes just not available in others. Houses for the most part had a pale-yellow hue, and as interesting as the adobe or stucco look was, by the end of the day, they all looked alike. Other structural homes consisting of brick or cement/wood siding looked interesting enough on the outside, but interior-wise proved to be disappointing. Our enthusiasm was slipping, and our apartment each time we returned after a day of house hunting grew smaller and smaller. The snoring intensified, the sleepless nights were multiplying, and I was completely restless.

Ironically, I planned my trip back to Wisconsin even before I left Wisconsin. However, at this point, time was not moving fast enough. Naps during the day seemed effective but out of character, and resting poolside outside was a health risk I wasn't willing to take. Being susceptible to sunburn kept me indoors. Early morning walks became my vice. Four-mile, five-mile, even six-mile hikes proved to be a form of relaxation. In sync with my music, I walked areas that bordered subdivisions on wide horse paths fragrant with plantings and flowers. Some areas warranted a nightly car ride back to check out the entire neighborhood with hopes of a house for sale. Others brought to my attention small outdoor malls with new opportunities to investigate.

A favorite pizza joint was discovered on one of my hikes along with a deli that we began visiting often for lunch. My son needed new venues to try out and sights to take in as well. Our beach runs always proved to be exciting, but the nights and weekends searching for a house were depleting everyone's enthusiasm. We upped our game and placed finding our

"Church Home" our priority. And from this priority came Saddleback Church, located in Lake Forest, CA. Listening to one great sermon after another generated a feeling of belonging far greater than anything else in the state. We had finally just discovered "home." This new find was a good thing. Church on Sunday followed by breakfast and then house hunting proved to be something to look forward to. However, for my son, this was a still a lowlight of the weekend, not the church, per se, but what happened after church. Driving around while sitting in the back seat of the Suburban. Every 18-year-old's dream, right?

We upped our game, and Saturday's challenge was now the hunt for great food and an activity, such as mountain biking, the ocean, and if all else failed, shopping. We also discovered Big Bear, a small town high in the mountains known for a ski hill. During the summer, you take the chairlift up and ride your mountain bike down. A risky conjecture of the unknowns for sure. Snakes, spiders, cliffs, and jagged rocks? No, thank you. I still preferred to travel by foot. Cal, however, enjoyed the adventure and asked to bring Kevin out to ride with him the next time. A perfect beginning of "bonding" with the new state.

Another work week rolled by, and Saturday, the day of house hunting, was again upon us. Dick had already mentioned that he was not available to help us, so it was up to us. This time, the sun played a role of getting Cal back into the car, for it was too hot to do anything else. He navigated the home search from the back seat with the air conditioning on. Food and air were the only two concerns for that day. Corona was our destination, amongst all the other thousands and thousands of cars heading in the same direction. The traffic was incredible, the heat was intense, even the temperature coming from the back with the air on was heating up the entire car. Cal, anxiously trying to find open houses on his cell phone, had sparks flying from his Android. Unfortunately, I couldn't assist; I could barely navigate my own cell phone to make an "Ok Google" request, and after five or six tries of this, I exhausted myself along with my family members sitting in the car with me. It was better that I left my phone at home, or just handed it off if it had more battery than anyone else's.

But today we were Corona-bound. Eleven miles away, equating to approximately an hour's worth of driving. Our attitudes were already melted into "this better be worth it." Of course it wasn't. The first and only house we had mapped out was supposed to have an open house that day; however, the listing agent was not there, and the house was not open. Yes, it just got hotter. And the days of putting in a video or handing over a juice box and pretzels were over. That was not going to be the antidote for the young adult in the back seat.

The pressure was on!!!! And from the back seat came the announcement of two new open houses in a town called

Norco, also known as Horsetown, USA. Wikipedia describes Norco as a city in Riverside County in the United States. And according to city ordinances, the architecture of Norco "shall reflect a desired Western theme," and it did. It also included qualities described as rural, informal, traditional, rustic, low-profile, and equestrian-oriented. The population of Norco was 27,000. Giddy up, let's go! We drove another 15 minutes or so and drove by what seemed to be a small shopping center with a Kohls, a grocery store, and other retailers, and on the opposite side of the street, a Starbucks, gas station, bank, and other entities. Looking good so far! The possibility that we could be onto something exciting once again was uplifting. As we drove up to the house, it was literally driving up a hill. We quickly parked, and quickly returned to the car within minutes. The asking price of the house was $839,000. And by the eluded comments made by the agents holding the house open, the owners had just moved out. My thoughts concluded that they moved out during the night with just a flashlight and forgot to take most of their personal items, including their own dirt and clothing lying on the floor. Wow, that was a shocker! We were completely blown away, and as we moseyed on back to the car, we waited for our next cue from the back seat. If not productive, this day was turning out to be somewhat comical in nature.

Still in Horsetown, USA, we were navigated to our next open house, taking roads that clearly sounded like we were on the *Gunsmoke* TV set. Dodge City Place, El Paso Dr., Thoroughbred Ln., Stirrup Way, and Gunsmoke Rd. We passed a CVS with a horse corral and an open space that seemed to be turning tumbleweeds. At the bottom of a slight hill, there was a park with a small play gym for children and a large fenced-in area for horses. And with all the horse paths came the horses. And literally, some homes had their horses in the front yard. From our car, we could hear neighing, along with the donkey and rooster noises – even though it was close to 3:00 p.m. The road we turned onto next curved, and as we approached the bend, we could see the for sale sign. We stopped in front of the house and gazed. We took a moment to think under the shade tree planted near the curb. We considered not getting out of the car, the house we just saw for $800,000 having been a shocker, and this could have been another. But nothing lost, nothing gained. We walked across the horse path, soft with sand, to the concrete driveway, up a slight incline, to the slate stairs and pathway leading to the front door. The palm trees swayed in the extreme heat, and the Mexican lavender was in full bloom. We reached the front patio where the water fountain sounded lively and refreshing, for this area was clearly defined as desert. The front door was open, and as we said, "Hello," and entered, a woman came forward with dark curly hair, wearing brown gabardine pants, and greeted us. I can easily recall the pants, and hair for that matter, for my mother always wanted me to wear the same brown pants, but truly, I preferred blue! And the hair, yes, I was finally growing mine out, and the longer it got, the curlier it got. Quite interesting.

Anyway, when she came forward, she said, "'Hello,' said the spider to the fly." Oh no, she didn't say that, that's in the next chapter. She said, "Hello," and introduced herself as Devlyn, the listing agent, and welcomed us in.

CHAPTER 12

"Welcome!" Said the Spider to the Fly

In the foyer, the beauty of the curved staircase with a dark stained wood railing and iron was captivating, and before you took to the stairs, your eyes followed the curve to the second floor. The open concept in the foyer emphasized the height of the ceilings. And it was like standing still for a moment. Refocusing our attention, we looked to the right at an incredible room with a pool table and a tribute to a family of athletes. This is where it was easy for me to see past this room and look beyond. Not a sports fanatic, I quickly moved on to an adjoined dining area with French doors that led out to the patio. Rounding the corner of the glass table and to the left was a butler's area, which introduced the kitchen. An unbelievable kitchen, which matched the picture of the dream kitchen I sent my husband months prior to our move. "Find me this," I wrote in the subject line. And attached was the photo that would make any woman want to cook. An incredible feat was just won! The kitchen resembled the emailed photo with all its amenities. An eight-foot granite island with seating, granite countertops and backsplash, spacious workspace, and abundant cabinetry to the ceiling. Stainless steel appliances, including a built-in refrigerator, gas cooktop, double oven, and a walk-in pantry. A dining area with views to the family room, patio, pool, and bar. There's a familiar movie that says, "You had me at hello." For me it was, "You had me with the kitchen." It was the kitchen of my dreams, the kitchen of the photo I sent to Keith, the place where I would be spending most of my day re-inventing myself. It remarkably contained the same granite as the granite I put in our home in Pewaukee and offered an unsurpassed likeness to what I was gravitating to: a relaxed Western style where we would blend in versus stick out.

Beyond the beautiful kitchen was an open family room, powder room, and laundry room spacious enough to hold my crafting creativity and more! A run of base cabinets and countertop extended beyond eight feet, and on the opposite side, more cabinets with room for a washer and dryer and a large utility sink with cabinet completed this space. I loved it.

There were two doors in the laundry room; one led to an extra deep two-car garage for cars, and the other to a two-car man cave, complete with a big black motorcycle, TV recliner, mirrors, punching bag, weight set, and man's best friend, a dog in a kennel. This couldn't have been more perfect. And I hadn't even made it to the second level.

Back in the house and onward to the second floor, a bonus room greeted you as you climbed to the top of the stairs. To the right of the bonus room was an unbelievably spacious master bedroom that engulfed you. Accompanied by his and her closets in a walkway to a huge soaking tub, toilet room, walk-in shower, and his and her vanities spaciously set apart by a large area that accompanied a bench in the middle of the room. Mirrors created the bigger-than-life image, but that is exactly what the master bath was.

The other half of the home brought you to a hallway with lower and upper cabinets, perhaps another eight-foot run with storage abound. Three additional bedrooms and a full bath created the balance to the master bedroom. And the bonus room, well, the bonus room was the natural place for a sitting area, TV room, or study.

Back down the stairs and to the left was a junior master suite with private bath. This room hosted a baby crib, queen bed, rocker, and dresser. And looking out through the plantation shutters, the fountain was in sight, and you could hear the sound of water splashing, again giving hope to the state of drought.

Wow, what else could a person ask for? Honestly, integrity and code of ethics never crossed my mind. Peace and tranquility did. I was looking for a home to restart my life. And in the home, peace, allowing my spirits to settle and my soul to be revived. But before that, all I could see was the home was decorated to the hilt, and the aroma of freshly baked cookies filled the air, chocolate chip cookies to be exact. Candles were burning, pictures on every wall, and a dog completed the staging of this home. And when my husband asked the price, I covered my ears with my hands, closed my eyes, and sang "la la la la" so I couldn't hear the response. So hopeful that we landed in a place that we could call home. I admit, I had already bought the house with my heart. Keith, however, was buying it with a mortgage, an investment in a new state of living, work, and home. Silence filled the room when the listing agent gave the price, then horns blew and confetti flew, for it was within our budget!

The world changed in the blink of an eye. This time, walking back to the car was different. It didn't seem as hot outside, the flowers were more beautiful and fragrant, and the traffic on the 91 was light. From there, my "Ok Google" didn't annoy anyone, but my excitement turned into anticipation which then turned into the dreaded fear of "what if?" What if someone else puts in an offer? What if someone puts in an offer today, tonight, or first thing in the morning? I can't say if it was my lip-biting or scrunched eyebrows, but my husband recognized the cue and said, "Let's go back and look at it again tomorrow." I could feel my shoulders drop and my neck relax as we headed back to that wonderful little apartment where my computer was on the snack bar and my bar stool was waiting for me. Waiting for me to connect to Zillow, but this time with an address. Yes, it's that merry-go-round of emotions, where the tickets are endless and hopping on and off is inevitable. Hang on, it's going to be quite the ride.

CHAPTER 13

Words That Begin with the Letter Z

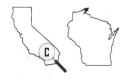

Zillow filled the 24-hour void until were able to drive back on Sunday to see the house again. Zillow's pictures and comments, especially on the $90,000 kitchen renovation, kept me entertained. The excitement of seeing the home again was thrilling. I could not wait. In my mind, I was already moving in. Unpacking, arranging and rearranging furniture, and making a nest was occupying my time. You see, I had been counting the days and complaining to my family about how upsetting my life had been. Coached by my oldest sibling, I was told to give it 90 days. And when I asked where the sound advice came from, I was told from a wise man, our father, who also once told my sibling the same advice. We both laughed, I cried, and then laughed again. I think I was on day 25.

This day, however, being Sunday, was a different day. We went to church, followed by breakfast, and immediately after that, we knew where we were headed. We had already calculated the miles the day before and the time it would take to get there. The address was already in our son's phone, and we looked forward to the sights and familiar path of yesterday. With the three of us back in the white Suburban, we headed west through the mountains and back into Horsetown, USA.

Sadly for Cal, the second visit to the house didn't include the cookies or even our agent Dick, but Devlyn, the agent who held the open house the day before, was there again. This time, she held the door open and greeted us with, "I knew you would be back." *Strange comment*, I thought, but I just went with it. This time, I noticed things had been changed. The portable air conditioner was now in the garage; the day before, it had been in the master bedroom. The candles were not all lit, and I could tell the carpet wasn't vacuumed like it was the day before. However, the same dead black fly was on the gas cooktop. I wasn't specifically looking for these items, my eye had just recently been trained to see them when I was preparing our house to show in Pewaukee. Which then made me wonder . . . *why aren't they packing up this 3900-square-foot house?* Each room except for one second-floor bedroom, which faced south, was fully decorated, floor to ceiling.

Could this be the way California stages a home? Hollywood

staging perhaps? Staging in Wisconsin meant you decluttered, removed personal pictures and possessions, and cleaned the canvas (so to speak), encouraging the prospective buyer to visualize themselves living in the home. It's incredibly interesting to say now that I didn't have the slightest clue what I was looking at back then. Was I wearing rose-colored glasses? Perhaps. Was I naïve? Sure. Was I hopeful that this was the house? You bet.

If you recall, our first experience was a builder giving us the combination to his house that he had on the market. The second experience was the ability to see a house without any realtor present. Our third house was recommended by our agent which didn't fit our desires, and lastly, the house with the open house the day after the sellers moved out was a complete and all-out disaster. I did have this overwhelming relief of finding something at that right price that I could call home. I did have questions throughout our second visit, and as I mentioned them to my husband, he responded with reasonable answers. I noticed as I meandered through the master bedroom on Saturday a unit on the floor in front of the master bed. He told me it was a portable air conditioner. That certainly made sense, but on Saturday, it was sitting in a large plastic container, perhaps in two inches of water, and on Sunday, it was in the man cave. Portable indeed. The massive-sized furniture in the room along with a number of other items left me somewhat perplexed. Not an armoire lover, or even a care in the world for a long dresser and mirror, I eyeballed the space and moved on to the master bath with the oversized soaking tub. In my head, I decorated the tub area immediately with soaking salts in beautiful glass containers, rolled plush white towels, an abundance of ivory candles, and the relaxing element of aroma therapy oils circulating in the air from my diffuser. The spa moment instantaneously relaxed my racing heart, and I was able to pull myself back to reality and headed back down the staircase.

At the bottom, I took a second look at the junior master bedroom and made my way to Devlyn to ask a couple of questions. The first, "Is the homeowner a decorator?" The agent replied, "No, but she likes to dabble in it." *Interesting*, I thought. Dabble is a word I never use, so it stuck with me. The only other reference to the home that Devlyn provided was that the family raised five kids here. How awesome is that? Right? Family is where lives begin and our stories evolve. It was all coming together; the house was large enough to hold my family, my siblings, and parents, my extended family, and friends of the family. It was going to be perfect! Already relaxed from the mental spa moment, the vision of family visiting and the potential of having our kids live with us again was all it took to ease the pain of the move. This was it; we had definitely found the home we wanted.

I was living in the moment in California, and for the first time getting back into the Suburban, the cabin pressure was different. Blue skies and sunshine for as far as the eye could see. The daunting task of house hunting just ended. A sigh of relief from my son and an opportunity for my husband to see me smile again gave us all hope that we could survive this move.

This is when the hypothetical movie director should have called, "Cut!" The audition is over. The candidates who currently walked on the set were a perfect fit (cue the white Suburban with Wisconsin license plates).

And from here the scene was set for the huge Ponzi scheme that was about to be unleashed. Yes, ironically, the house captured the hunters. Unbeknownst to us, the family from Wisconsin just auditioned for a hellish rodeo ride of a lifetime.

CHAPTER 14

Purchased with Heart

I fell in love with the home; I could visualize the excitement this would bring to my own kids. The home was spacious and perfect for entertaining, and the backyard offered all the amenities young adults would be looking for. A pool, spa, grill and bar, along with swaying palm trees and a portable Bose speaker for music. It would be perfect! And for my husband, a garage all to himself. A man cave, workout station, and/or place to find an antique car and commence rebuilding. On top of that, the home was in a quiet neighborhood, had views of the mountains, and was semi-private. I didn't have to sell Keith on the home, it sold itself. He saw a happy wife, which equated to a happy life. And yes, this house had *the* kitchen. The kitchen my move to California hinged on.

The home was surrounded by palm trees, a water fountain, beautiful landscaping, and a view of the mountains; it was picturesque. Add a horse path, the scent of the California pepper trees, a split rail fence, and the fact that it was nestled in a rural-like area, I thought this was as close to perfect as we were going to get. We contacted Dick once again, and instead of having him continue our search, we told him we had found *the one*! With excitement surpassing anything else so far in California, we felt we were onto something great.

Yes, were all incredibly excited, and even more enthusiastic, when Dick said he would meet with us that evening and write our offer. He suggested meeting us at a little tea and coffee shop in Yorba Linda, just 10 minutes away. The idea of putting an offer on the house was thrilling to me. My wheels were spinning. As we headed across town, my brain was already miles ahead of myself. If we put in our offer, and it's not accepted, then what? Over the weekend, did someone else write an offer on the home? Was it accepted? Oh dear, I thought I had packed all the possible stress one could hold just from the move alone, but I was wrong. I was gathering more stress as I vigilantly looked for the tea and coffee shop. And when it finally appeared, it was on a corner with the open sign illuminated indicating available parking in the back. Excitement beyond all possible belief was now holding my chin up, and my eyes were as wide as gumballs. It was like calling out, "Bingo!" to a crowd of 38 million, saying we found the house!!!! But every winning card has that moment of calling back the numbers to verify, and that moment before the announcement of "Yes, you have Bingo, and yes, you are a winner" was killing me.

But not to worry, this was a house we were putting an offer on, not a chip on a Bingo card. And we were working with a real estate agent, not a Bingo caller. However, thinking back, he never did read back the numbers, or indicate what the prize was really comprised of. Dick wrote down the numbers in the contract, asked for our signatures, and said he would forward it on to the listing agent, Devlyn. Dick mentioned he had once lived in Corona, which was approximately a stone's skip away, and would eventually get in to see the house we just wrote an offer on. Our meeting ended within 30 minutes, and our drive back to the apartment seemed to have taken less than five. Three days later, we were still wondering what the outcome would be. Did we get the house or not? A 24-hour day somehow miraculously transformed into what seemed like a week. I had to find a channel to release all my nervous energy, and I started walking again. I would start those walks around 8:30 in the morning and return around 11:00 a.m., calmer, and with more freckles. One would have thought that the energy put out during the day would exhaust me at night and I would have a peaceful sleep. However, just the opposite. Exhausted by

7:00 p.m., but wide-awake again at 10:00 p.m., I had plenty of time to listen to my husband snore and see my son glow in the dark because his phone would light up his face with every text message received.

By now my hair was beyond shoulder-length, and I had to ask myself, was it truly growing or was I pulling it out? The overtired-but-can't-sleep syndrome left me extremely exhausted. But by morning, I was up for another seven-mile hike, different path, but same stride. I started out in whatever direction put the sun at my back. The freckles, however, were still accumulating, and I had the appearance of a full-fledged tan and natural highlights from the sun. Life was full of surprises at this point. So surprising that on one of my walks, the phone rang, and I found out our offer was being countered. We also countered, and within hours, our offer was accepted. Did I sleep well that evening? The answer is no.

CHAPTER 15

Four Eyes

Morning came, and the decision to walk seven miles was now trumped by the decision to take a ride out to the house that we had an accepted offer on and check out more of the area. In doing so, my son and I just so happened to see two GE service trucks near the driveway of what was to be our new home. This was interesting because there was not an appliance concern checked on the seller property questionnaire or the transfer disclosure statement. An indication, then, that all major systems of the house were in working order. These two reports would be similar in nature to Wisconsin's real estate condition report. Again, a lengthy report of direct questions pertaining to the property's condition that each seller is asked to fill out disclosing notice or knowledge. So back to my question, what could the reason be for the trucks? It couldn't be the washer or dryer because neither were on the property, nor included in the offer. All that was left was the stainless built-in refrigerator, double oven, dishwasher, and gas cooktop.

I made this my first question on inspection day, which was Saturday. Dick gave us a recommendation for a home inspector; it was a friend who he went to school with. The inspection would normally take four hours or so, and we were told to arrive at the last hour for a review. When we arrived, the listing agent Devlyn, the inspector Dennis, and Dick were gathered in the kitchen. After kind introductions, I asked the question of the day. What were the two GE service trucks doing at the house this past week? Undeniably a shocker to Devlyn, for all eyes went to her waiting for her response. She said she knew nothing about that and would ask the *sellers* and get back to us. As we continued to chat with Dennis, we discovered that he and his wife, Mara, welcomed a new baby the night before and, though she was still in the hospital, he was still able to help us. We were obviously thankful, but understandably sad, and a little surprised, that we took him away from his new family. But if that wasn't already enough of an uncomfortable feeling, Dick requested a discount on the price of the inspection while we were all still gathered in the kitchen. This made me and my husband cringe. Dick mentioned he had a coupon but forgot to bring it. Dennis awkwardly made it sound like the coupon had already expired, and with this in the air, it was uncomfortable even breathing. The first of many awkward moments to come.

The conversations continued, and we discovered that this was the first day Dick had seen the house. However, both agents did a visual inspection of their own and each noted no major issues or concerns. Dick's report included black markings on a mirror and a sticky door jam. Devlyn's report was quite similar, indicating in writing, **"All good."** So good, that Dick said to Dennis, "No matter what, they are going to love it!" We felt we couldn't have been in better hands. Dennis's report indicated an electrical outlet under the sink that needed a plate, along with several others. One of the two air conditioner units may need a charge, perhaps adding freon, because of its age and was recommended for further inspection. The attic furnace units needed attention, perhaps maintenance. An electrician would need to update and bring to code an outlet hanging loosely in the attic. Other than that, Devlyn was going to find out where the screens were and why two service trucks were at the house. Conversations continued, and as the clock ticked to 4:00 p.m., we questioned where the termite inspector was. He was apparently running late for his appointment. Devlyn said she would hang behind and see if he showed up and would then contact Dick. With regards to the appliances, if any repairs were made, our agent asked that receipts of work be provided.

The following day, Devlyn contacted Dick and said the termite inspector arrived later that evening, and the report, which was then forwarded to us, was clean. Things were progressing. The service trucks apparently replaced a door gasket on the freezer door of the stainless built-in refrigerator. And the screens we asked about were in the garage. The seller took them off to not have an obstructed view to the pool. The air conditioner was serviced, and what was to follow next was a date given for a final walk-through. With an accepted offer, accepted inspection report, financing in order, final walk-through date and closing date verified, a trip to the mountains to relax was in order.

The ocean one day, the mountains the next. We were literally going to be living in the middle of both. I stopped counting the days for I knew I wasn't going to reach 90. Each day until closing, I had the urge to drive by the home, but I also filled that time with walking and finding new and interesting places for lunch. I often browsed the infamous HomeGoods store and checked out other nearby hot spots. And, of course, when we did drive by the house, my radar took in all the details, including a stake truck in the driveway. A stake truck? Are they moving themselves out of a 3900-square-foot house? A stake truck, with wooden sides, exposing everything as it starts rolling down the road? Obviously, they were not moving far, and perhaps not taking the freeway. For the floral arrangement of dried goods in a brown vase packed immediately behind the driver's seat in the open bed of the truck would not have made it very far.

On another occasion, after returning from the mountains, a display of free furniture was left at the end of the drive. A sale had just concluded, and what was left was free. Oh, how I wish I had stopped. But I think my kids, for our older son was also with us for the weekend, would have had a field day with me. We planned a trip to the mountains to ride bikes and hike. And when returning from the miles and miles of hiking and bumps and bruises from spills on the bikes, I asked if we could take a 10-minute detour and drive by the house again, and surprisingly enough, everyone agreed! This time, I noticed a small-framed woman with blonde hair walking a dog that resembled the dog we saw kenneled during our showing. *Awesome*, I thought to myself, *all is good for me*. The homeowner has blonde hair, loves her animal enough to walk it, and enjoys decorating. I took this in as all good vibes. Buying this house was like buying someone's else's story. I needed to feel a connection, a sense of happiness radiating from the house. I took all of this in, and everything looked promising.

The anticipation was starting to get to me. The ability to pack up the apartment was joyous! Picking up my apples and reformulating my life was going to be adventurous. Starting up a new home décor business or seeing what I could do to offer my art to local retailers was beginning to take over much of the time that once was filled with worry and uneasiness. However, less worry did not increase my sleep. If I left anything behind in Pewaukee, it was my sleep pattern. A consistent, solid five to six hours a night was all I needed, but now I was lucky if I got a solid three. Napping for 20 to 30 minutes helped, but that "radar" thing never allowed me to totally shut down, for I never wanted to miss a thing, including phone calls. But very rarely did my phone ring. I still found myself hoping for invitations to lunch or for someone to show me the area or take me to a favorite attraction or invite us over for dinner. I was hopeful for a girls day out with our banker, an invitation for a glass of wine with a neighbor, or even a call from my husband's work to invite me in for a tour or even dinner some evening. Not the case. I was, however, invited to that baby shower!

CHAPTER 16

Closing Day

Hip hip hooray, it's closing day! We signed contracts at Starbucks one sunny morning on the patio amongst lattes and cappuccinos. I was dumbstruck at the selected location, but I was trying to learn to just go with it in California. And the key to our future happiness was all happening today. No agents or even keys for that matter, for Dick directed us to meet him at 2:00 p.m. at our new home. I never considered why our agent and keys were not at the closing, I guess they wanted the time to prepare the house, just for us, and that they sure did!!!! Cal and I jumped in the car, and at exactly 2:00, we were at the house. We could tell by the cars parked outside that Dick was already there, along with the carpet cleaning service. A house-warming gift from our agent. We entered through the garage, and on the kitchen counter sat some realtor koozie sleeves and gray t-shirts. Dick greeted us, handed over the keys while commenting how I was not going to like the condition the house was left in, and made his way to exit. I think as he pulled away in his Lexus, he kicked up enough dust to hopefully make him and his auto disappear.

He was right, the house was a mess. They must have just completed their move that day, leaving no time to truly remove everything. Even the obvious black fly on the cooktop remained. The kitchen cabinets still had dishes, the pantry had trails of food, money was left in drawers, a subwoofer sat above the double ovens, and a contractor list and miscellaneous items were left everywhere. Brackets were left on some walls, while not on others. Décor items were left on high shelves and in areas clearly out of sight. It was disappointing. Upstairs in the master bath, a grimy oil residue ring coated the spa, and cups of samples perhaps from Massage Envy lined the medicine cabinets. His side of the master bath delivered black hair from razor clippings, a used Band-Aid of all things, floss sticks, small rubber bands, and more hair. On her side, there were sample-sized lotions and oils along with other makeup. The kids bath left more of the same, including earrings and long black hair that had to be snaked out of the drains. The house now unveiled what the staging concealed. The garage held the window screens all torn, perhaps from the dog scratching at the screens to get in? The small bell at the back door for the dog to ring to go out assisted with this conclusion. A dog that has to go out has to come back in. The garage shelves were full of old paint cans and stains which I had requested to be removed. More toys, children's art, and miscellaneous junk was found. Outside of the garage and towards the front patio, more elements of décor remained. An old bench painted turquoise blue had an old real estate lockbox attached, covered in cobwebs. Ironically, this house never had a lockbox on the front door. At each open house, Devlyn was there to let us in. And she was also there to let us in for our home inspection, even when we were accompanied by our agent and inspector. And if you recall, Devlyn also said she would stay behind for the termite inspector and didn't ask our agent to stay and lock up.

In the backyard, dog toys and water dishes remained along with lots of undisposed items, including dog waste. *Crap,* I thought. Quite literally. I just sold our home and cleaned until the moving truck came. It was cleaned to the best that I could offer, for when we left, we left our name behind, and my name as a decorator, so I wanted it to be perfect, absolutely perfect. I cleaned each room floor to ceiling and everything in between and would finish by closing the door behind me. The day of moving, when the washer and dryer were changed out from the buyer wanting both units to the buyer bringing their own,

I ran out and borrowed my neighbor's paintbrush to paint the area behind the machines that were no longer there. I can't say I left anything unattended, and I think my kids would have agreed. The look I was going for was "Did a family of four really live here?" Could one even tell we raised two boys here? The last of the items in our garage to be removed were Woody and Buzz action figures from the movie *Toy Story*. They guarded our garage, and now were packed to guard our next. But this new garage had glitter and stickers, and evidence that little people lived on the property, or perhaps visited often? The glitter made me think it was little girls, and I remembered seeing the family portraits, so I was pretty sure my guess was correct.

Before I could move in, I had to clean. And as the carpet cleaner was sweating his life away upstairs, he commented that he wasn't told the actual square footage of the carpet; so much more than he had bargained for was laid out in front of him. He pointed out a water stain on the carpet in the master bedroom, ironically where a rug once laid and where a portable air conditioner sat. The reveal was clearly the reason for the oddly placed rug, and now with the large armoire and rug removed, what was unveiled was damaged carpet. Under the carpet, mold, and behind the baseboard trim on the drywall, more mold. Instinctively, I knew the rug and large furniture in the room was oddly placed, but to each his own, I assumed.

The portable air conditioner seen once in the bedroom and then removed to the man cave was also odd but noted.

In the kids room where Devlyn asked if the sellers could leave behind a "new box spring and mattress" was an old box spring and mattress dated 2005. It was torn and soiled and rested against the wall. It was not new, as she had offered. And what appeared behind the box spring and mattress when I pulled them away from the wall was a hole in the drywall the size of a fist. In the next bedroom over was a quick-fix plaster job, taped and lightly mudded, but haphazardly done. It was still damp, so I took it off, and it revealed a larger grapefruit-size whole. Nice attempt, but poor craftsmanship.

Back in the kitchen downstairs, the receipt for the refrigerator repair was on the counter. Sure enough, it indicated a new door gasket was installed. The receipt was for $75.00, and I saved it. The request for the air conditioner and furnace service noted during our inspection was also confirmed by our agent prior to closing, and though a receipt was emailed to him, it was not printed out and left for us. By now, I had rummaged through all the drawers and doors of all the cabinetry and stockpiled the left-behind belongings. Outside I did the same. The back patio had numerous items, which included an old baker's rack that rested against the back side of the house. Perhaps it was forgotten, or just too heavy to move. A large planter hung on the wooden fence dividing our property from our neighbor's, along with a tin washtub used as a planter which sat just below on the ground. The flowers that were around the pool were now just empty pots. Yes, the owners took the flowers. And the pool, without the pump running, didn't create the spa-like setting that once looked so inviting. The whole aura changed.

The temperature was hot outside no doubt, but my internal body temperature was beginning to rise as well. When we had enough for the day, my son and I went to close the garage door, and it did not work. We noted that in our inspection but were told it did not operate because it was too hot from being in the direct sun. I never said I was a genius or electrician for that matter, but all I had to do was adjust the sensor "eyes" and the door closed!

We were headed back through the mountains, and back to the little apartment which too had changed. It was now just a launching pad, two days and counting. Our moving truck was scheduled to load and deliver the next day, and our move-in date would be Saturday, August 22nd. Until then, I cleaned and collected what the original owners left behind, including that little black fly that was so insignificant, until it wasn't. The following day, we watched as the movers reloaded the moving truck from our storage unit, and after 20 miles or so, unloaded it all into each designated room of the new house. The process of unloading the boxes from the garage seemed less daunting.

The larger furniture pieces were directed and placed exactly where I had envisioned, but from the garage, I could prioritize what needed to be unpacked next without overloading the main floor with boxes. Next, we would move our tiny, little apartment goods and ourselves.

CHAPTER 17

Driving Home

Move-in day came, and as eager as my husband was to rent the U-Haul to move the apartment furnishings, I was as confidently eager to drive to our new house by myself. My attempt two days prior, with my son as my passenger, proved to be an all-out disaster. I took the wrong exit, which turned into a full-blown meltdown. That was the day my son called his father for a 911 visit to the house. It was one of those days where anticipation turned into disappointment and disbelief. Tears rolled faster than the traffic, and my cheeks were soaked with no signs of a reprieve ahead. It wasn't necessarily that I took a wrong turn, but perhaps that I wasn't supposed to have left Wisconsin at all.

Yes, Keith drove out from work, consoled and supported me. Remarkably, everything seemed better. So, off to another run at it, and yes, I missed the exit again. This time, I drove one exit too far, but now considered it to be an adventure. A detour to check out more of my surroundings. No one else knew it but me (well, now you do too). I toured another part of the area and made it back to my main street and home minutes before the U-Haul. This was truly move-in day. The movers had already unloaded the semi the day before, and what was left in the garage became a process of one box in, emptied, flattened box out, repeat. This made the process simple and agreeable to all. By midafternoon, we had our first visitors. Two men on horses stopped to welcome us. *Incredible*, I thought, smiling widely. *This is amazing.* I couldn't have been more surprised. Was this really the reality of living in Horsetown, USA? Yes, yes, yes. Horse paths instead of sidewalks, visitors on horseback vs. car or bike, and neighbors that came to welcome us. Better yet, they were two co-workers of my husband's, one of which lived only a street away with his wife and two kids approximately the same ages as ours. The other gentleman, also a co-worker, was just out for a visit. This truly had been an exciting day. We had horses growing up, but we never did visit a neighbor on them. Oddly enough, our property allowed horses, according to the listing agent, but our backyard was a hill. I wouldn't know where I would put one if I could. The riders trotted off, and I was my usual busy self, unpacking, making beds, and writing a grocery list in my head.

At this point, I had no idea if my helpers (husband and son) were in the pool, playing pool, or running an errand to stock the bar outside. All I was focused on was making this house ours. We purchased some of the items from the sellers, including the pool table, high-top table, chairs in the kitchen, and an entry table. The additional pieces of furniture, along with our own, gave us a great start to filling the rooms. The pool table room, which was once filled with sports memorabilia, trophies, plaques, and photos floor to ceiling was now just walls discolored by the sun and nails left where pictures once hung. *I'm not concerned,* I thought as I eyed it up, though it was the biggest room on the main floor. I knew the whole house needed paint. From the mis-measured stripes to the faux painting that must have been experimental, I planned on painting it all. And while unpacking each room, I was taking notes, a to-do list if you will, for what my vision of each room would be. I let the kids pick their rooms, and with two guest rooms still available, I found myself drifting off into my favorite time of year, when family or guests would come to visit. Yes, Christmastime. A permanent Christmas room on the second floor would be just the ticket. And on the first floor, the junior master bedroom would be a *relaxed Western retreat,* authentic to Norco. But with each room came additional discoveries, beyond the house just needing paint.

By day four, I was typing a letter to our agent Dick explaining our disappointment in what we uncovered. We requested the old box spring and mattress they left behind get picked up. And the list rambled on with holes in the walls, the unswept condition, the items left in the house, along with unwanted debris in the yard, the paint cans and stains that remained, and more. We also needed the repair receipt on the air conditioner unit. Outside, my husband was busy trying to figure out the sprinkler system. A concern we both shared, for the sprinklers were going off between four and six times a day. California was in a drought and the city had water restraints, yet everywhere on our property, water was springing up, front yard as well as back. At this point, I was hoping no one would notice that we lived here. I tried calling the city's water department to find out past water bills, but they would not offer those to me. And truly, I was more concerned about our future bills. And the hotter it got, the sound of the sprinklers and water displays made me want to hide out in the backyard. In the backyard, I had no clue as to what we were watering, but the hillside was plush with greenery followed by one or two flowering lilies, yellow in color, happily planted next to a huge rock. The backyard was concrete the length of the house, and from there, the pool and spa occupied the space followed by the great hill and tree line, and beyond that, another hill and fence.

Days rolled like tumbleweed from one to the next without any response from Devlyn or her firm, and the feeling was like living in a ghost town. All who were actively present in the beginning of our transaction suddenly vanished once the property closed. Not quite sure what to do, I started my 7:00 a.m. phone calls to my sister Kate in Northern California.

The following week, we were planning on taking Cal to college. The changes were happening faster than the seasons; diapers to college seemed overnight. On move-in day, we had a short drive just an hour and 15 minutes straight south. I was hopeful it would be easy to navigate, and it was. Cal would be starting his freshman year, and my husband and I would start living as empty nesters. Yikes!!!!

I just entered another complete and unfamiliar territory. My emotional roller coaster had peaked where I thought it couldn't go any higher or lower. Since I was dropping off my son at school in a new city, I decided to spend a full day studying the area myself. Trying to take it all in was like discovering a whole new community, for a third time. First the apartment, then Norco, and now his college community. I was going to miss him dearly. We had just spent the last 20 months together. We experienced things only he and I could relate to. Losing our dog Marlo was our greatest loss, and living on Laureate Drive in Wisconsin alone was our greatest achievement, along with surviving the apartment.

I was clueless about living with one son in California now starting college while having my older son in Wisconsin, completing his junior year. It was like playing Twister, and I was stretched. Trying to keep a hand and foot in Wisconsin while living in California was tough, but we all adapted. And what came to mind the day we dropped off Cal at college was the maturity I saw in him for the first time. He wasn't the baby in the family anymore. Maybe I was. Much of what we experienced was difficult. Change is difficult. I clearly didn't have it all together. We dropped our son off, and on our way back, I became more focused. Street signs and off ramps became more important. I was studying the directions, planning the impromptu visits, and considering all the ways to stay connected to my son and his new school.

It was a somber drive home, and as we pulled up to the house, you could hear a pin drop. The garage door opened, and there sat Buzz and Woody. What was left of our kids' childhood sat on the shelf and welcomed us home. It was now just the two of us, and yet one more was planning to leave. Keith was preparing for work on Monday and had mentally left hours ago. For myself, I was just trying to figure out my next move, and my question, a big one, was "What on Earth am I here for?" Why all these changes, and what am I supposed to do with all of this now? Morning came, and my husband left the house at 5:30 a.m. His return, perhaps 6:00 p.m. During the hours in between, I talked on the phone and studied my Facebook page. Day two proved to be more exciting. I talked on the phone, studied my Facebook page, and planned a remodel to the guest room with private bath. By day three, I talked on the phone, studied my Facebook page, and recognized the house needed more than a guest suite remodel.

It was now over a week of living at the house with just the two of us. Quiet evenings and cooler nights were upon us. One evening after dinner, while sitting in the family room with my husband, strange noises rang out from the kitchen. We heard a clicking sound behind the granite backsplash, and a moaning, grinding sound from the refrigerator. We both looked at each in puzzlement and thought, *Did you hear that?* Without another sound or call for action, we got up and walked over toward the noise. The clicking noise came from an outlet, and the refrigerator was making all sorts of noise. The new door gasket was not doing the trick. The door was covered in condensation, and the ice was melting. "Do you still have the GE receipt?" "Sure, I do," I replied. I gave it to Keith. The receipt had two phone numbers electronically printed along with the warranty of the service call. When he called the first number, we were both quite surprised. Inadvertently, it was not the GE service number, it was the seller's cell phone number and, after a moment of conversation, Keith apologized for the call and hung up. We looked at the receipt again and found the GE service number. We gave them our address, and they replied that this call would fall within their 30-day service warranty, and they would come back out. Great, in the meantime, we will just keep an eye on it.

At night, Keith and I would often take walks, engaging in conversation about the exciting things that happened during the day and what our plans would be for the following day or weekend. Our street was dark, illuminated by our neighbors exterior lighting and our own, making the walks flashlight-worthy. We often walked around the block, sometimes resting at the highest point while soaking up the beautiful lights from the surrounding communities. Evenings were peaceful, quiet, and filled with soft breezes, but ever so warm. One evening as we were walking up our street and closing in on our home, a helicopter flew overhead, lower than normal, and louder than I've ever heard before. But it wasn't the noise that startled us, it was the bright light encircling us as we stood looking up wondering what the hell was happening. We didn't know if we were the target or if there was someone else out there they were searching for. I was too scared to move at that moment, yet somehow, I still ended up in Keith's arms. We waited for the helicopter to remove the light and carry on before we took our first step. And then I raced back to the house and collapsed on the sofa. I've only seen this happen in movies, but we are in California, so welcome to the new norm?

Experiencing everything I could put a spin on things like never ever before! Welcome to the Wild Wild West! Included in this wild adventure were the streets and city life that looked like we moved back in time to the dusty trails of authentic cowboy life. Folks from 'round these parts rode their horses to the liquor store and to CVS. Street signs for "stop ahead" had a second tier, with a picture of a horse and rider and the words WHOA! Crosswalks were equipped with two buttons, one to reach at pedestrian height and the second if you were on horseback. I stepped outside our house one day to check on the water in the water fountain and noticed a horse with a saddle trotting up the path in front of me without its rider. I was stunned at first, but then I immediately took off hopeful that I could try to stop it, flip flops and all. Off to a great start, it was a sudden fail. There was no way I could have caught the horse in flip flops, and when I turned back, I noticed the rider walking along as if in no hurry and heard her say, "He's heading back to the stable." *Ok*, I thought. And I moseyed on with my day. If I was going to fit in, I had to learn the lingo. I also quickly learned that if you wore a cowboy hat, you received better service than if you didn't have one on, and if you said "Howdy" to people on their horses, they would often stop and talk to you.

I had one lady approach our house on horseback and heard her call out, "Friend or Foe?" What was that code for? She must have seen me behind the bush that I was trimming. I stood up and said, "Friend." We chatted for 20 minutes or more, and I discovered she sold things on Etsy. I was eager to look into that and wondered if I could change my mindset and sell items on Etsy as well. Of course, during this time I was also thinking that I needed a horse too. Unfortunately, I still didn't have an area to put one. The city later informed me that the listing advertisement stating that horses were allowed on our property was incorrect; we could not have a horse.

So, no horse. But, I did notice I had a white and yellow cat in our backyard. I watched her ever so gingerly walk the retaining wall until she leaped to the edge of the spa to take a drink. I didn't like the idea of her drinking chlorine water, so I surrendered my yellow Tupperware dish and filled it with fresh water. To silence her cries, I also decided to give her some food. I didn't have any tuna in the house, but perhaps a little turkey would do. I climbed up the right side of our steep hill next to the iron rail fence which separated us from our neighbors and placed the turkey on the ground. Hopeful that the cat would find it, I went back into the house and carried on with my day. Later in the evening, I checked on the turkey, which had, unfortunately, turned to jerky. I tossed the turkey and put fresh water in the yellow bowl. If the cat returned, I planned to add tuna to my grocery list. I had found a purpose, a cat to care for.

The cat, perhaps, was a much-needed distraction. It allowed something other than a "material" thing to occupy my time; it was a reprieve. A reprieve from the noise coming from the walls and refrigerator, the sprinklers and garbage left behind. Focus on the positive. Focus on the cat. And let someone else focus on the strange noises.

The first appointment was welcoming the GE Appliance repairman back for a home visit. Originally, he said he was going to arrive between the hours of 3:00 and 5:00 p.m. I also called our agent Dick and asked if he could stop out and bring three complete copies of our contract. He said he would arrive around 6:00 p.m. Ironically, they both arrived at the same time. The GE repair man told us that he told the previous owner that this GE refrigeration unit was junk. He told the owner a door gasket on the freezer door was not going to fix the problem, but a door gasket was ordered and installed anyway. A $75.00 bill helped them escape an $11,000 replacement. At least that was how it initially appeared.

This was simply the kickoff to the deluge of events that continued to unfold. As the repairman left, I am sure Dick wanted to be in uniform as well and depart right along with him. Hearing what just transpired left a coolness hanging in our kitchen. And over the weekend, my sister Kate revealed that the house we purchased used to be a rental. She noted the property questionnaire was manually filled out but electronically signed. I had no idea what that meant, other than she was just bringing it to my attention. The three copies of contracts were to ensure that Kate received one, along with our need for a complete packet ourselves and for the potential need in the future. The idea that the house was a rental property contradicted the contracts that indicated the property was seller-occupied. We asked Dick how this could have been missed, and he said he did not look at the MLS regarding this property. As if that wasn't puzzling enough, he also added that he would help where he could, but he did not want to tarnish his record as a realtor and he would not go to mediation.

Mediation, what is mediation? This week was going to be one hell of a week. I scheduled lots of visitors, including an electrician, the heating and air conditioning company who serviced our units per our contract, and painters, who painted the house in 2013. How did I know which painters to contact? The paint cans remaining were from a very familiar paint store. Each label had an account, and each account had a connection to either a contractor or designer. Why all of this in a week? Well, I was leaving for Wisconsin the following week and wanted to inquire about everything so I could be worry-free once I boarded the plane. I also wanted to concentrate on how I was going to entertain my husband's boss's wife, Ruth. Yes, after the baby shower, I returned an invite and asked if she would like to fly in and spend a week with me at the Wisconsin lake house rental, and she accepted.

By mid-morning the following day, the electrician came and pointed out areas that needed to be addressed. The noise coming from the back of the granite in the kitchen, and other notable entries made earlier on our inspection report, were all going to be taken care of. Great. In the afternoon, the HVAC company came and said we had a gas leak in the attic, and one of our air-conditioning units would soon need to be replaced; it was no longer serviceable. Wait, our request for service or repairs was part of our contract, and our agent said it was taken care of. What do we do now? And by Friday of that week, the painters had conveyed that the previous homeowners had had a big leak in their second-floor bath, and it ran down the exterior wall in the foyer. If it wasn't already hot outside, things were certainly heating up inside. Wait, let me revisit the property questionnaire report. Absolutely no problems noted with the house, present or past. And on the Agent Visual Inspection Report, the same. What were these people looking at? And why was the report manually filled out and then electronically signed by the seller? Or maybe the question should be "Who filled out the seller property questionnaire?" I continued reviewing the piles of paperwork and discovered, as well, the termite inspection report was a copy of a previous report, out-of-date. And when I called to see if it was recorded, it never was.

The home warranty company sent a plumber to address the gas leak in the attic and said we were lucky. But not so lucky with the HVAC tech. The HVAC tech said we would need a new AC unit and told us we would only get one to three years out of our current unit. He also brought to my attention that the house did not have a whole house fan as advertised in the listing brochure. Perplexed, anxious, and saddened by all of this, I tried various visits to the city of Norco to look for house plans, permits, and history on the home. House plans, yes. Permits, no. The additional electrical work to the man cave, family room, and laundry room produced a big zero.

I called the home warranty company regarding the refrigerator, but for some reason, the built-in refrigerator was not added as an upgrade when the home warranty was ordered. Now what? Despite the holes in the walls, the dirty box spring and mattress, and piles of what seemed to be worthless contracts sitting on my counter, I now had a refrigerator that kept the refrigerator side cold, but left the freezer side dripping with sweat.

The letter Dick wrote to Devlyn and her firm spelled out our concerns, but was a complete fail. Dick himself also disagreed with us, saying we knew the house was tenant-occupied. Yes, we argued about that find daily. Dick said we knew at our home inspection that the house was a rental. But Devlyn was there, she could have cleared the air immediately, and she didn't. She did not disclose what she knew, and our agent did not investigate what should have been obvious to research. Instead, was the mission to covet the commission? I heard that saying from someone, and it resonated with me.

I continued with my own investigation and discovered

that Devlyn was also the daughter of the tenants, who were the original owners. And when we mentioned this to Dick on the phone one evening, he said he couldn't believe it. He said he sat with her through the whole home inspection, and they chatted for hours, and she never mentioned that her parents were the original owners. We also told Dick that the sellers (who were actually the renters) had sold the house in a short sale in 2010 but had continued to live on the property as renters. And by means of convenience, the original owners/renters were bought out by Devlyn's father's employer. And the company which employs Devlyn's father holds contracts with the state of California for road repair. Hence the stake truck owned by the company and used by the original owner/tenant/employee was used to help move. But wait, the house that was sold in a short sale still had the original owners living in it? Yes. And the listing agent, who was the daughter of the original owners who sold the house to us, also lived in the house during the time it was on the market and didn't disclose such facts? Yes. And she didn't know the refrigerator was junk? Correct. She denied everything. Remember when I noticed that the pool table room had family photos and trophy memorabilia? Somehow I had an inkling that one of the five kids in those photos, all now adults, was the listing agent. Was this my woman's intuition? But if you recall, I also mentioned the woman walking the dog had blonde hair, and these four girls had dark. Interesting, very interesting.

CHAPTER 18

24 Hours in a Day

Yes, there are still 24 hours in a day, and each day my husband went to work, I went to work and did what came naturally. Yes, it is true. I woke up one morning and decided to be an investigator. My laundry room held my computer, and after each 7:00 a.m. phone call to Kate, I keyed away at my computer. Incredible information was a sip and a keystroke away. Black coffee in one hand and my scrolling mouse in another. Literally, the Moon and the Stars were aligning.

I called the escrow company after discovering that the property was tenant-occupied. The escrow officer on the other end of the phone said I was not to question her position and ability to do her job and hung up on me. It was the same escrow officer who took us out of her office and into a hallway to answer questions we had prior to our closing. Perhaps the document in my hand from the escrow company identifying the title to the estate and vested interest of husband and wife as joint tenants was correct, but was it truly sold as an income property? And did it concern anyone other than me that we signed contracts stating seller-occupied when it truly wasn't? The names on the deed of trust to secure an indebtedness- short sale—in the amount of $376,000 on November 9, 2010 and recorded on November 15, 2010—listed Devlyn's father's employer and employer's wife's name as the purchasers of the home. However, the employer and his wife never lived on the property they purchased, for they own their own estate worth millions near San Diego. They only wished for us to believe that they occupied this residence. The HVAC invoice with the employer's wife's signature which was misspelled was one of many clues. Instead this employer bailed out the original owner/employee and allowed them to stay and to continue to live in the home. How do you reason with that? But wait, there's more.

One afternoon, I decided that if we needed a new air conditioner, it would be best to see what was out there, and for that reason, I decided to gather information directly from the source. I looked up the address of the HVAC company and added that to my list of stops. My first stop, however, was Target, for pool-friendly dinnerware and plastic cups. If you do your

"A" priorities first, then the rest of the day is yours! I jumped in my white Suburban, backed out of the garage, and headed south up our street to the stop sign, hung a left, and headed east.

As I proceeded east, a white Kia four-door sedan passed me, with a red "Kia of Irvine" cardboard license plate attached to the front. Why so much attention to this car? White just happens to be my car color of choice, and it looked like a possible contender for me to purchase a smaller car since I no longer needed cargo space for my store, kids' sporting goods, or even another move. A sedan perhaps, and that Kia truly piqued my interest. Up the big hill and down to a stop sign, the streets in Norco were exciting and quite adventurous. Especially following the roads to Hidden Valley Golf Course, which was five minutes from our house and was the most majestic course I have seen. The mountains surrounded this little town and gave me a feeling of being nestled in a large state. Solely concentrating on my directions, I approached Target, entered the parking lot, and what to my wondering eyes should appear but the white Kia. *Interesting!* I thought. *They must have immediately turned around to approach the store basically at the same time I did. How coincidental!* I parked, grabbed my purse, and quickly walked across the black asphalt parking lot and into the store. This must be an affirmation of the car I am to buy. The "see it, like it, and consider wanting one, then you'll begin to see it everywhere" phenomenon.

Once inside Target, I barely made it past the Starbucks. Coffee has always been my weakness; it helps me power through my day and gives me clarity. I already had four or five cups in for the day, so I placed my eyes on another distraction – the dollar spot. First the rows of silliness, and then on to what I came to shop for: plastic cups, dinner and sandwich plates, and anything else that could have jumped in my cart as I cruised through the aisles quickly, but alert. After I checked out, I quickly checked my to-do list. My next stop was not quite as exciting. I was going to check on a new air conditioner unit. I walked to the exit, where the sliding glass doors opened and a wave of heat hit me. Between the heat and the yellow haze that lingered over the steamy asphalt, I walked back to my car and hopped in. A short 25- to 30-minute Target run left the black seats of my Suburban hot and sticky, making it uncomfortable to sit. I needed the air on and proceeded with asking OnStar for directions to my next stop, the HVAC company.

By now, OnStar and me should have been on a first-name basis; however, they continued their professional and courteous service by formally addressing me and assisting me with turn-by-turn directions. As I proceeded to my next stop, I recall noticing that OnStar had me pull into a small strip mall. Neither the building nor the space were recognizable. I did not see any signage or clue that I was in the right place. I parked, facing the door to which was supposed to have been the correct address, and hopped out and peered into a glass door that was locked. A man appeared and said the HVAC company had moved and was now located one block north and one block west. As I turned around to head to the new location, my eyes turned to the car parked right next to me. It was the white Kia, in a space close enough where I should have been able to see the driver if they were still in the car, but oddly, I could not. The windows were tinted heavily, and my window-knocking career had not yet started. I just simply hopped back into my car, took off in the direction the gentleman told me, and arrived by luck at the HVAC building. I had to call this time to make sure I was in the right place. Again, no signage, but the woman on the other end of the phone described the building for me to go in to. I parked facing the street, and with the building now behind me, I hopped out, walked across the lot, and entered through the double glass doors. As I entered the lobby, I easily could have turned left or right, but opted left. I could see a bench close to the back wall and, further down the hall, cubicles with office desks. Again, I'm thinking, *Am I in the right place?* A woman called out and asked if she could help me, and I said yes. As I approached her desk, I said, "I am here to look at replacing my current AC unit, and I was hoping to see and compare units that you carry." The woman informed me this wasn't a showroom, just the office.

As I looked up and out of the glass windows, a white Kia drove in. I could feel my eyes widen. I thanked the woman and returned to the bench in the lobby where I sat down and fumbled for my keys in my purse. I had to see if this individual would come into the building, and I had to see who it was. Shortly, she appeared. As she walked in, she didn't pause to determine the direction to go in, she immediately turned left and walked right past me. She approached the same woman sitting at her desk. I listened. I first heard my heart thumping in my chest, and then I heard the Kia woman ask, "What was that woman doing here?" In that moment, I was asking myself, "What in the hell am I doing here? Why was that woman following me?" And from here, the list of questions and uncertainty beyond uncertainty began to run through my mind. Could it be the listing agent's sister? Her complexion was darker, she had dark hair, and was very close to my height. Similar looks, but no, it couldn't be her sister. Our listing agent and her siblings all had to have been pushing 5'8" or taller.

I don't remember how I stood up or even walked back out to my car. The adrenaline was flowing, and my body was shaking. The palms of my hands were instantly sweaty, and my blood must have gone straight to my heart rather than my brain. It was fight or flight, and I was not standing still. I got back into my car, backed up, and drove aimlessly out of one parking lot and into another. Which parking lot or off what street, I had no idea. I just pulled into a large office parking lot and turned my car around so I would be facing out to see any cars wishing to turn in. I called Keith. In a panicky voice, shaking beyond belief, I cried out my fears that someone was following me. He told me not to worry and refocused my attention and direction to help me find my way home. He also reminded me that I was heading back to Wisconsin the following day and said that while I would be in Wisconsin, he would visit the Kia of Irvine dealership and would ask who could have been driving the car.

The next day, I enlisted myself in my very own witness protection program and couldn't wait. Early morning flights had become our specialty, but not our favorite. With this flight scheduled to leave at 6:00 a.m., we had to be up by 4:00 a.m. "Enlisting in my very own witness protection program" was Kate's humor, and I loved it. But it wasn't enough to keep my mind off what totally left me perplexed. Why would someone want to follow me? What purpose would they have? If anything, if someone tried to follow me while I was in Wisconsin, I think they would have given up. Potentially, I could have made 10 stops in a day on average. But here in California, the risk of not knowing where I was going would have truly exhausted the other person. The wrong turns, toll roads, traveling in the right lane only, and forced right-lane exits even exhausted *me*. Desperately trying to refocus my thoughts back on Wisconsin, I started counting down the hours until I landed. Back to familiar surroundings, good friends, and the possibility of a little relaxation. A good friend picked me up, and as we drove off, I called out, "Back to the lake house, Jayne!" and we tooled off in her dark blue Lexus, the car filling with chatter and laughter. I knew what the following days would bring. Family, friends, sewing projects, art projects, and gazing out at the lake. The lake brought me a sense of calmness, even more so than my new state with its proximity to the ocean.

CHAPTER 19

Batman and Robin

Yes, the daring experience of moving to California brought me back home within 76 days for a long stay, and I loved it. My friend (and the sewing machine she brought with her) gave me all the distractions I needed. Fall was slowly announcing its arrival as the leaves changed colors and cooler air moved in. The calmness of the lake in the mornings and afternoons was picturesque. And by the weekend, the lake would be waving to those standing on the shoreline. Pontoon boats at a slow cruise navigated around the speed boats pulling skiers and the paddleboarders putting their core to the challenge as a result of the ripple effect. My perspective of the ocean vs. lake had changed already. The ocean, mighty and magnificent, left my peripheral vision with concernment. The constant urge to look over my shoulder beyond the waves in front of me became more of my concern. The lake, however, less in mass but greater in significance, left me looking right with neighbors and left with purposeful living. This incredible reprieve was already providing me serenity. Lasting moments of happiness vs. fleeing moments of uncertainty. Optimism started filling my 45-day Wisconsin vacation. I picked up my life where I left off, and it was exciting. As for the white Kia . . . it was thousands of miles away.

I sewed and painted and worked out. I entertained, and for the first time felt as though I had hopped off the tour bus and was touring Wisconsin. Why now? Partially because I never really made time for myself, and secondly because now I had all the time in the world. With the ability to rent the familiar lake house, a sense of peace came back into my life. And the thrill of sharing it with a friend from California was going to be double the excitement. The lake house and my dad's black Mercedes. Yes, I was back in the saddle, and not on a horse in Norco.

The old saying of give it 90 days, well, I had to start counting again. Perhaps the white Kia put the emphasis back on counting, but on day 79, I was happy to say I was driving to the Madison airport to pick up my husband's boss's wife, Ruth. A new experience all its own. Have I ever driven to the Dane County airport? NO. Was the day scheduled for adventure beyond helping others with their decorating needs? Yes. Am

I a beer drinker? No. But the thought of doing what everyone else was doing in Wisconsin sounded wonderful, so after I successfully picked Ruth up, we ventured off to the New Glarus Brewing Company. A self-guided tour explained as much as I wanted to know, and the pint of beer at the end was quite quenching. I'm not a beer lover by any means, but I gave it my best. We purchased trinkets and beer signs and made our way back through the countryside, to I-94, and finally back to the lake house. So far so good, except that I had planned salmon for dinner. Though she wasn't a fan, we managed to sip through a few cocktails, which kept the fun on course. Whiskey sours became my new favorite drink, mixed and shared with my new California friend. By Thursday of that week, we were invited to join the Ladies of the Round Table for breakfast. It consisted of nourishment, coffee, and conversation and happened each Thursday at a local restaurant in Brookfield. When we lived in Wisconsin, I had attended quite infrequently due to work, but on many occasions when my Thursday timing did correspond with their, the togetherness felt like a big hug. Always supportive and encouraging of one another, it was the group of all groups to be a part of. So, this particular Thursday, I wasn't going to miss out. It was an opportunity to connect with my dear friends, and we went. From there, we stopped at a friend's home which I had decorated, and from there, motored on to getting fuel. I also decided to run the car through the car wash.

And much to my surprise, the sunroof leaked. Laughter sprang from the car much like the water from the ceiling. Completely baffled as to what leak to stop first, I tried both hands to the ceiling, but it wasn't going to do the trick. Ruth, now slightly dampened, eagerly donated her denim shirt, and we laughed until the car wash door opened and the dryer went on, then we laughed even harder.

Those were the moments that I thought made our friendship. We continued to tool around that week in my dad's car, and I personally couldn't have been happier. I've referenced that black Mercedes twice while writing this book; I think that car really comforted me. It gave me the feeling of security as the miles rolled on, as a tourist of the state versus a resident.

We painted during the day and sipped whiskey sours by day and night. Using watercolors, painting for fun, and relaxing was a first for me. Enjoyment and satisfaction filled my life like never before. Pontoon boat rides, whiskey sours, pontoon boat rides, and more whiskey sours flowed like water over a dam, effortlessly. And little by little, it was all going to be ok when I returned to California. Over the weekend, we had a party at the lake house to celebrate my parents' birthdays. We invited all my family – aunts and uncle, nieces and nephews, we all shared in family time. My husband, however, was not in attendance, and I think he started to become concerned that he wouldn't be able to lure me back "home" after all this family time. Well, he did it. He purchased Zac Brown tickets at the Hollywood Bowl in LA. Brilliant idea! My favorite band, and something exciting for me to think about. My return trip was going to be the start of our big adventure. We were out of the apartment, in our home, and our younger son was off to college. The idea of heading back to California was more favorable than ever before.

Ruth and I had a great week, and after I dropped her back off at the airport, I filled my remaining days with projects. The days in Wisconsin went by faster than I anticipated, and the one project that was supposed to have been completed didn't ship in time, therefore the install of the shades was delayed and so was my return trip. I stayed two extra days, completed everything work-related, and enjoyed the company of my good friend Ella who took me back to the airport. This would be my first return trip to California, and I hopped out of the Volvo with optimism and excitement. I just surpassed my expectations of entertaining a complete stranger for a week, and I didn't have a worry in the world that my husband wouldn't have checked into the white Kia. If the complete opposite would have occurred, Ella would have had to park her car and literally pull me out of it. She already knew of the days when we were in the apartment and experienced the walks I took and frustration that went with each mile. Perhaps we both felt that this departure was going to be the real start of living in California. The excitement of flying in the same day of the Zac Brown concert helped me to focus on the positive and look forward to greatness. All was looking up until the plane landed. I hopped into our car and asked my husband, "Did you happen to find any information on the white Kia?" First, he paused, then said, "No." Then he paused longer. I think I just tripped over my own heart. Was this the start to our new adventure? Or was it cause for an all-out war?

Wasn't I worth looking into it? My heart-rate monitor, if I had one, would have exploded at this time. The feeling of disbelief swallowed up the relief I felt in Wisconsin instantly. I immediately regressed to counting this as another day closer to 90. The feeling of uneasiness crept in as my husband's two-letter word settled in. I buckled the seat belt around me, and it felt like the only protection I had. Welcome back to California!

I breathed in and out slowly and tried not to allow this to disrupt what was happening in six hours in LA that day. But within the same six hours, I could fly back to Wisconsin and Ella would be there to pick me up. It was fight or flight. And I was still at the airport, creeping our way through traffic. But what was really happening seemed out of my control; it was the beginning of the number eleven wrinkles forming near my eyes and nose. Frown lines followed, and the need for antacids became a new staple. What seemed like a 45-day retreat was wiped away in 45 minutes or less! However, trying to stay positive and looking on the bright side of things, I had a new friend, Zac Brown concert tickets, and the opportunity to choose to be happy. The concert was incredible, the weather was outstanding, and I was back in California with Keith and Cal.

My return to Norco must have alerted the cat to have the rest of the family of feral cats welcome me home. One by one, the family came forward, and now I had five cats sitting on our retaining wall. All adorable and entertaining. Each day, like clockwork, they appeared. And each evening, they sat on the wall staring at Keith and me, as we did the same to them. I named them and found the friendliest to be Joe, the dad. The mom, Tabitha, hissed at me, and the three kittens were timid and shy. Cat food became a grocery staple. I knew better than to friend feral cats, but I couldn't resist. Everyone needs someone they can count on.

It was now the middle of October. I was looking forward to hosting our first Thanksgiving and invited my husband's parents and my sister and her family. And as our house concerns grew greater, we considered hiring an attorney. Someone who could assist with our home discoveries. Our own attempt to send a letter to the real estate office and actual sellers, regarding further discovery of undisclosed issues, proved to be useless. We received a letter from the real estate company saying they were not obligated to mediate or arbitrate and declined to do so. Obligation is between buyer and seller, and seller was not responding. The walls, however, did. I painted everything I could, which lifted my spirits and took me to heights up to 24 feet. I graced the open staircase with paint, which curved to the second floor and ever so carefully laddered the walls onward and upward. Eighteen gallons of paint brought the house to how I wanted to see it. Interior first and later exterior. Subtle colors, calming yet powerful, left simple beauty, hiding nothing and uniting everything. One color, for the entire first floor, opened the rooms. I wanted a guest room for tranquility and a master bedroom for a retreat. I wanted the kitchen to be welcoming and the dining room to be adorned with family first, then color. The family room had to be inclusive and the bedrooms reflective of peace. I finally let myself benefit from the talent of which I fervently worked so hard on and sold to others. I poured myself into this house and bathed it with paint and purified it with sage. Thank you, Jayne, for the sage. I secretly wished I could have smoked something similar in nature, but I was happy to smoke my home.

By late October, California looked the same. I could not tell that fall was upon us. The temperature was the same, and the leaves were not changing colors. As I continued my daily routines and adventures, I became keen to my surroundings and people around me. If I stood out, it was because I had Wisconsin license plates and my Wisconsin accent. But when others stood out, it was because they grabbed my attention, like the man I saw at the hardware store not too far from my house one morning. He was a tall man, clean-cut, blue jeans, white shirt, and cowboy boots. He was looking in the same aisle as I was, but not picking anything up. I was curious. What was he doing here? And even more interesting . . . he was outside at the same time I was, getting into a silver pickup. Events such as this kept me on my toes. Throughout the week, I would entertain myself with daily drives and to check out new venues, such as music in the park, restaurants, and various grocery stores. One area of our town was home to a Boot Barn, The Watering Wheel tavern, a parking lot for cars and its very own corral for horses. Truly, this town looked like a set from *Gunsmoke*, and several of the characters reminded me of Fester. Yes, you could ride your horse to town to shop, dine, or drink. Trot on over to the Saddle-Sore Saloon and you could tie your horse up while you tied one on. An incredible community which undeniably lived up to its name, Horsetown, USA. Pickup trucks were everywhere, and driving my white Suburban made me feel a part of the pack.

When the weekends arrived, I put the paintbrush down and enjoyed spending time with Keith. I often took him back to interesting spots I found during the week. On one particular Saturday morning, I took him to an interesting grocery store located next to the Boot Barn. I had discovered an authentic Mexican grocery, and perhaps soon a fantastic hot spot to shop when the kids would come for a visit. But what appeared outside as we left made an alarm go off in my head. Not this again. The hair on my arms stood straight up. A chill ran down my neck despite the 100-degree temperature outside. A tall man standing left of the doors was leaning against a pickup truck with his left leg up against the bumper, cowboy boots and all, and was talking on his cell phone in a foreign language. I just saw this same man yesterday at the local hardware store, in the same clothes. It didn't seem like a coincidence. I wished I had kept up with my Spanish so I could understand what he was saying. But besides that, my real intuition was telling me something else was happening. It would be best to nonchalantly mention it to my husband, and not to ruminate over it.

Momentum was building with the house, more history of the house was being discovered, and my new profession as an investigator made for more coffee being poured as I pored over more and more information.

CHAPTER 20

Poking the California Bear

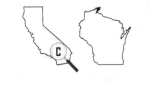

The weekends were the easiest to conquer. Keith was home, and our activity list was endless, and of course if Cal came home, I had more than plenty to do. Laundry and grocery shopping and more laundry. During the week, I tried to stay focused. Remodeling the junior master bath started one morning, and that led to a day trip to a local ReStore where I donated a sink and countertop. This was my first excursion by myself to a small town approximately 24 miles away. Leaving the sink and countertop outside next to our green and black garbage bins would be a strong hint that something was happening inside the house. I didn't know if Keith would have objected, but since I didn't tell him what my "workday" looked like, I just went with it. I found success in small day trips. I was then motivated to visit more home improvement stores, and with the next one just being eight miles away, I became a frequent visitor. I began researching products and people. Remodeling the bath with one hand and picking up a magnifying glass with the other.

I often wonder why I was so interested in continually searching for negative information. I'm not quite sure if I was spending more time remodeling or keying away at names and addresses on my computer. I do know that I'm better at multitasking, and by doing so am more creative. Either way, I wanted to be digging into the specifics of the short sale in 2010, the reason the lockbox was still attached to the blue bench, and why, according to one neighbor, no one was allowed in to see the house. Staged to sell, but never shown to sell. The bank wanted $470,000, but the employer, a high school football buddy of the original owner/tenant, was able to purchase it for $376,000. But wait, there's more. I don't think someone counted the number of bedrooms, garage spaces, or even indicated the house had a pool when listing the home during the short sale. Oh, what a web we weave.

And by now I had called the heating and air-conditioning company to come back out for a third time and look at the AC. And this too raised an eyebrow. If you recall at the time of our home inspection, we were instructed to "request: review/ repair or servicing by a qualified HVAC tech." And our agent Dick along with Devlyn were present and fully assured us that this would be completed prior to our close date, and it was. But I was astonished to learn from the HVAC tech who chatted with me at our kitchen table that a coupon for service was rendered for a $75.00 tune-up. He also said the listing agent and homeowner, a *blonde-haired* woman, were both present on the property during the inspection. And when the tech asked to go into the attic, they both refused to let him. The requested homeowner's signature on the receipt for the tune-up was also misspelled. Misspelled, meaning the employer's wife's name was misspelled. The tech told me the blonde-haired woman signed the receipt. The tenant, acting as the seller, signed the employer's wife's name. The HVAC person also identified that the seller opted to pay in cash. And ironically, when the invoice for the work completed was emailed, it went to the listing agent's mother's email address, and not to the actual seller's email address. Confused? You may be at this time, but I felt I was hot on the trail of fraud. However, at the same time, I was poking the bear.

By now, I didn't even have to go out to a store to find something unusual, for it began to park in front of my house. Every day, a silver car parked in front of my house on the right side of the street. Doing the right thing sometimes takes courage, which then makes fear the scapegoat if you don't follow through. I also reasoned with myself that I already traveled too far, in my opinion, and invested too much to walk away from what my future was going to hold. Peace is what we were looking for – and certainly within our home.

But peace of mind did not park outside my house every day, a certain silver vehicle did. Curious, I often looked out the window for answers. But all I could see was a cigarette hanging from the lips of a woman with dirty blonde/brunette hair which was faded by the sun. She occasionally held a fountain drink and perhaps did some stretching exercises as she stood at the back of the car. It doesn't really sound like I had anything to worry about, right? Unless, of course, you would notice that it's always in the same spot, and always in front of my house? I did try calling the police to check out this car, but due to a high volume of calls to the police station, a squad did not arrive in time to address the vehicle. So as days followed, I gathered the courage to approach the vehicle myself. When I nonchalantly asked what she was doing one day, she replied that she was taking a break before heading to work and mentioned she worked at the day care at the bottom of the hill. Interesting. Yes, there is a school, but it's not at the bottom of the hill. The school, and perhaps day care, is two streets away with parking allowed on both sides of the streets. I knew because I walked that area several times a week. I returned to the house and continued with my usual routine – having no routine at all.

By now, the weather was beginning to change, and yes, the leaves were finally transitioning in color, and though it looked like a start to a fall day, it was really the end of November. Time to decorate for the holidays? At this point, it all seemed like too much work and was no longer a passion. I finally felt what some of my clients might have felt when they hired me to trim their tree or decorate their homes. My enthusiasm to decorate dropped to zero, and my creative energy was zapped. I was too preoccupied discovering the bad that I couldn't even engage my creative side to create the good. And with that attitude, moving forward into December resembled every other day here. If I had a burst of energy, I posted it on Facebook. Cutting down a birch tree in my backyard was one incident of that. However, cutting through the extension cord powering the electric chain saw stalled any further activity or creativity for that matter.

But if one day was ultimately going to be different, it was the 10th of December, my birthday. I had big plans for my birthday with my friend Ruth. This friend relationship was different than I had originally envisioned. An on-again, off-again relationship that led me to believe that she really wasn't enjoying life or was too busy with life and enjoying it all immensely, like I once had. We texted occasionally and since September may have gotten together once or twice. Unfortunately, I think trying to be optimistic with this new friendship was my pitfall. I believed that since she was my husband's boss's wife, this relationship was supposed to be wonderful! But it left me defenseless. Her nephew was the agent who assisted us in buying the house, and ultimately, the more I discovered, the harder it was not to complain about the house or about the nephew. Where was he anyway? I think not wanting to "tarnish his record" left him wiping this transaction clean. After he dropped off the three copies of the contracts, which were barely legible, I could only envision him driving off and giving us the forever goodbye wave.

On my birthday, Ruth arrived around 10:00 a.m., and within minutes of standing in my kitchen, she gave me an envelope to open. An envelope her husband had given her that he got from their nephew Dick. There was no name on the envelope, but once I opened it, I saw immediately it was a "Dear Aunt and Uncle" note in which he was expressing his appreciation for their referral with a wad of hundred-dollar bills. I knew the card was not intended for me. And as I handed it back, my heart sank. Ruth and her husband were being rewarded for someone else's bad performance, and it was at the expense of my husband and me. Call it what you will: a bird dog fee, a referral fee, an illegal fee paid to an unlicensed agent fee. I think the nephew gave the card to his uncle with the intention of paying a referral fee. And he mis-interpreted the message and thought he was supposed to give it to Ally . . .

I froze at the thought of what just transpired. I hoped and wished for an explanation, yet my "friend" was silent. Clearly my investigative skills should have kicked in and I should have taken a picture of the card and counted the cash. Instead, I gave it back and wanted to move back to Wisconsin! Why was this happening???? And, of course, I didn't say a word and proceeded to pretend life was great, but by now, I knew it wasn't.

We drove to a town hosting a holiday craft fair, and I spent those moments trying to recover from the morning. After lunch, we drove back home to Norco, and after she dropped me off, I couldn't dial my cell phone fast enough. I explained to my sister Kate what just happened. By now, the series of unfortunate events continued to gain momentum. I couldn't get back to Wisconsin for Christmas fast enough, and "Home for the Holidays" was never going to be this one.

With the holidays fast approaching, I tried desperately to get into the spirit and baked Christmas cookies to share with my neighbors. We had had very little conversation with our neighbors to the right since we moved in, so bringing them some homemade cookies was an interesting experience to say the least. Literally, the Mrs. wore sunglasses and pretended not to see me wave daily as she took her son to school. She often put her right hand up to her face to block her side profile view as she drove by and then turned right into her driveway. And the only conversation we had when we moved in was when I asked her if she was going to see the previous owners soon or had a phone number for them. I mentioned they left a lot of things behind, and she said she was having dinner with them that evening. She also made one other comment when I apologized regarding my air compressor making too much noise on a Saturday morning. Her comment was brief, "You decorate, too!" Seems to me she knew her previous neighbors pretty well.

My neighbors to my left were already defensive when we moved in because they had mentioned that they previously had a break-in and were uncomfortable with us asking questions about the previous owners. However, they smiled when I gave them cookies. Slowly, we engaged in conversations, and eventually, Rose and Walter became friends. Our neighbors one street over, however, were a different story. When I knocked on their door to deliver cookies, she didn't recognize me. Her husband worked with mine, and though we had met before, I had to explain who I was. Very awkward, but it too gave me a better sense of how to respond positively to make a better connection. We eventually started going out for dinner, dining at each other's homes, and we walked our doggies together. Yes, it all could have been better, but I complained a lot. Cher said it best, "If I could turn back time." Yes, I am positive I would have had a better run at this whole California experience if someone wouldn't have thrown a stick in my spoke. Head over tea kettle? Yes, however, it prompted me to start using my left brain. I was now a new CSI show – changing the name from *Crime Scene Investigation* to *California's Scrappy Investigator*.

The listing agent, Devlyn, may have a degree in forensic science, but I have had this "radar" thing going for me long before she was even born.

On December 21st, Cal and I hopped on a flight back to Wisconsin. Spending valuable time with my parents was key, and being able to visit one of my dear older friends was priceless. My dad and I drove over to Appleton on the 24th of December, stopping at a Costco for last-minute gifts, Kohl's for a book, and a care facility to visit a very dear elderly friend of mine. The visit became a vivid realization that we were all getting older, and "time together" was a priceless gift we gave each other. My elderly friend's spirits were lifted that day that I came to visit. She remembered me and gave me a hug like no other. She whispered in my ear, and tears welled up in my eyes. Leaving her that afternoon as she watched out the window broke my heart. "Keep 'er Cool" was her favorite line, and I repeat those words when I'm in great despair. It's ironic, for what wasn't purchased on that trip became my greatest gift to give. Time! My friend passed away in February 2016, but her strong, dynamic persona lives on in me. I will forever remember looking back while moving forward at the same time. The rearview mirror captured "life." And time became the most valued gift we didn't shop for, but were given.

The Christmas spirit was finally upon me, and I had already moved past our Thanksgiving experience. Our first holiday to host turned into an unequivocal disaster. As soon as my in-laws walked in, I quickly tried to outline what was happening with the house. In fact, I think they had just barely stepped inside the front door when I unloaded my heartache to them.

I probably talked nonstop for the first 10 minutes, and their reply made my jaw drop. My father-in-law asked when Keith would be home. Ahhhh what??? My first thought and lasting thought was *Didn't you just hear my heart speak to you?* How was I supposed to entertain guests or even think of having a good night's rest with that going on? I think in hindsight, I needed a parent figure, or another version of an adult to hear and respond to my woes. I needed a hug and to hear it was all going to be ok. But in lieu of that, I heard, "When will Keith be home?" My heart broke, and my relationship with my in-laws galloped off in the wrong direction.

I just gave up everything to move out here, and I started to feel more than my home falling apart; I was falling apart. The only thing coming together was the search, revealing more and more about the home. Again, with no parent reprimands I swore like a pirate – a Pewaukee Pirate who was now more consumed with finding the bad than searching for treasures.

Our agent Dick should have noticed all of this obvious information simply by being attentive and looking at the MLS. He also underestimated the results of this error. By now, the ball of yarn which was attached to our agent's foot when he handed over the keys had unraveled faster than one could ever imagine. The closeness to my friend Ruth, aunt to our agent, was slowly eroding as well. Trust, as solid as it sounds, has the word "rust" in it. And my tears of frustration and disappointment were eating away at the bond we had developed. She was my only sidekick in California, and I wasn't sure what the true meaning of our relationship was, only that it felt like I was getting kicked in the side, and it was deliberate.

We celebrated Christmas with my family in our small Wisconsin town, then continued to the lake house where we celebrated through the New Year. 2016 was going to be exciting! My return trip wasn't scheduled until the tail end of January, and with that known, I had plenty of time on my hands and I could gather my senses. By mid-month, I made the decision to move forward and filed a request for mediation. Corresponding with the Bureau of Real Estate confirmed my decision. This nightmare has got to end. The past few months of revealed secrets wasn't the end-all. I may have slowed my role of investigating, but more information trickled in on its own. Mail with the listing agent's name started arriving in our mailbox, and not junk mail, but mail from a financial institution. Mail also arrived with the original owner's names, and never the employers. The employer operated several businesses and held contracts with the state of California. But no mail ever arrived identifying that they ever lived here. Only the listing agent and her parents. If I had to explain the staging of the house, it accommodated the needs of the listing agent/mother of three. The need for a crib, bunk beds, and a themed SpongeBob SquarePants room along with so many other areas described what the house looked like raising kids and not grown adults in their twenties and thirties. A first-floor closet was painted like a small play area, and clouds painted on the ceiling of another bedroom gave the likeness that children occupied those rooms. Perhaps it was also what was left behind: trinkets, sprinkles of glitter and crafty items, earrings and lotions, and small toys noted in earlier chapters.

Keith and I took a stroll to the mailbox when we first moved in, allowing me to have my first encounter with our neighbor to our left. I only bet if I know I'm going to win, and that day, I made a bet that the listing agent was part of the family that lived in the house, and that she in fact lived in the house during the time it was on the market. If I was correct, my husband would do the dishes for a week, and if I was wrong, they were all mine (and we would eat out). So, I asked the neighbor if the listing agent lived at the house. He nodded but didn't speak. I think the neighbor was more surprised no one had told us this.

The walk back to the house took forever. The weight of his response on my mind began to slow me down. What else were we not told? Obviously, a lot more, or why have someone follow me, right? But my goal for this new year was to regain my faith and believe that this whole situation would clear up once we attended mediation. The attorney we hired was to aid us in the resolution with some restitution or rescind the house. At this time, I wasn't sure if I was supposed to get my law degree or a realtor's license. I was compelled to find answers to my questions, and though my husband listened to me and either nodded or verbally agreed, he didn't fuel my fire to search further. I stoked my own fire, along with my sister and our 7:00 a.m. phone calls. Coffee in one hand, phone in the other. Stress, heartache, and the pain of restless nights and lack of sleep can erode a body from the inside out. My eyesight was also heading south, caused, I'm sure, by keeping an eye on the fire that sucked the life out of me. Either way, I now needed cheaters to read what the real cheaters were writing! But I had to look forward. It was now time to fly back to California. Off to another run at it. I enjoyed the flight with my son, and it is true, when you have a diversion from what ails you, life is so much better.

CHAPTER 21

Football Fool

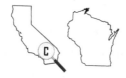

Diversions, it's what I needed. We slowly reformulated our approach to our neighbors on the left and focused on common interests. We started seeing movies and engaging as neighbors. The fence line that separated our lots didn't seem as visible anymore, and lunch engagements, casino runs, and a little decorating gave us all a new direction. My husband and I started attending an evening class at a well-known church in Lake Forest called Saddleback, and it literally helped me get back on the saddle of living. Attending a weekly program allowed us to encounter a new "table" of friends. We started attending more events, including music in the parks, and often drove into Orange to see a band that played at Ruby's, a restaurant and bar near the train station. Making the effort to enjoy more of life seemed effortless at the time. Family and more friends came out to spend time with us, and for that reason alone, the house with five bedrooms served its purpose. Entertainment wasn't something we had to go out and seek either, for when family arrived, we entertained each other. I was able to showcase my driving skills to my aunt Lola, a retired schoolteacher and real estate agent, and to my uncle Buster, who once drove a semi for a living. My uncle Buster always chose to sit behind me in the passenger seat. I was never curious as to why, but later I caught on. My uncle Buster asked me if I could see him through my rearview mirror. I said, "No," and he said, "I know you can't," and chuckled his little laugh. The rearview mirror was for my lipstick. I was still only concentrating on the traffic ahead of me and to my left and right. My goal was staying focused on my lane (the middle one). All my time spent in the far right lane took me on far too many exits. However, the middle lane was far more terrifying for it was legal to lane split if you were driving a motorcycle. Aunt Lola clinging onto to her seat must have felt the concern. And I think we both chuckled when I said that I needed a bumper sticker that said, "Big-Ass Suburban from Wisconsin, stay back." Either that or school bus stop sign arms that would swing out, indicating if I wanted to turn left and one if I wanted to turn right.

Soon I had to give up my Wisconsin license plates, which was truly another an eye-opener. Taking away my Wisconsin plates was like taking away my right to drive slowly and with my turn signals on. It was now time to blend in. To get my California driver's license, I had to take a written test as well as what seemed like providing 12 forms of ID, and my Wisconsin driver's license was not one of them. I pulled up to the DMV and parked on the side of the street. Upon getting out of my Suburban, a pickup truck pulled right up behind me. What got out of that truck made me pinch myself. A real-life cowboy hopped out! Complete with hat, jacket, cowboy boots, and spurs. Where am I again? Those were the moments that made me smile, while the rest of my California life made me cringe.

We were invited to a Super Bowl party – Broncos vs. Panthers. Finally, the luck of having boys paid off big-time, and I chuckled as I continued to get dressed that day. I had a Carolina Panthers jersey to wear, which belonged to Kevin, and I was ready to tackle a full viewing of the game like never before, and literally like never ever before! Yes, Ruth invited us, and we picked up a bucket of Buffalo Wild Wings and headed west. A party with some familiar faces made the event seem enjoyable, but when sitting down next to my friend and her husband, the temperature changed immediately in the room, and I wondered why we came. Why was an invitation extended when it was intended for one not to come? That was my question. Awkward moments lasted the entire first half. I exchanged the halftime show for a time-out and joined a woman who announced that a home décor store had just opened. What a short-lived save that was! The Panthers lost, and by the next day, I was on my way to losing another battle with the home warranty company.

I called the home warranty company again and asked why the refrigerator was not included in the package. Was it because a door gasket was added? No, I was told the refrigerator was not included because the built-in refrigerator was never checked on the order to begin with. What? The home warranty, offered with the home, was ordered by our agent, not the listing agent, and not checked. I called the number on the GE receipt again, but this time, I had to provide a name on the account. Customer service informed me that the name on the original receipt had since been changed and the cell phone number was also removed. By now, my detective skills had even impressed me. I knew I could guess the new name they used for the account. The maiden name of the previous owner, AKA tenant. I was correct. I needed to inquire more about the refrigerator and its history. How many times was it serviced, and by whom and when? You see, this should have been all disclosed to us on the seller disclosure statement, and it wasn't.

Interesting, very interesting. Call me Jessica Fletcher, or call me incredibly intuitive, but whatever you do, don't tell me that I didn't warn you about our 500-800 talents that God has gifted us with.

However, the real kicker to the home warranty contract was that Ruth had ordered it. The aunt to our agent, and my husband's boss's wife. Yes! And each time my husband would chat with his employer, the disbelief of how the refrigerator was omitted from the warranty came into play. My husband had these conversations long before we discovered who placed the order. $H?T! And the roller-coaster ride at this California amusement park continues. The ups and the downs came faster as time progressed, and the feelings of frustration kept climbing and never ended.

Entertaining guests was still a distraction, until I dragged them into the water to swim with the sharks. Fleeting moments of living the warm California life came and went as fast as the service at our local In-N-Out Burger. What was really beginning to stick were the pounds caused by cortisol in my body. I was a cortisol producing machine, and my nerves were shot. Weekly, I would retreat to Keith's walk-in closet, plug in my phone, and iron my life away while chatting with my girlfriends in Wisconsin. Average number of daily phone calls to friends: 2. Average number of phone calls per day to parents: 3. Average number of calls to inquire about our home: 5. Average number of phone calls made to my sister Kate: 10. What you focus on . . . expands. Together, we were now a new CSI show. Not *CSI: Miami*, *CSI: Norco*. California Sisters Investigating Norco! We impressed each other daily with our finds. We were good, but wise to the concept of "who really cares?" Maybe I should let someone else focus on this whole ordeal. Keith hired an attorney in December, and she thought it best to move forward with mediation. Her number one concern was that the listing agent had advertised the property with a $90,000 kitchen renovation on Zillow. I'm already thinking... are you kidding me? That's what you're going after? I believed the sale should have never happened. What about the short sale and no-arms-length transaction? Shouldn't the focus be on the illegal transaction of selling a home and allowing the original owners to remain on the property? Followed by the original owners engaging their daughter as the new agent to sell the property when she lived there and didn't fully disclose it? What seemed liked mountains to me were incidental tumbleweeds to our attorney.

CHAPTER 22

Mediation or Plain Old Mediocrity

Considering the results of what could come from it, I evaluated the purpose of mediation. Mediation is a non-adversarial confidential process that brings disputing parties together with a neutral, unbiased third party (mediator) who assists the parties in reaching a mutually agreeable settlement of the dispute. The mediator does not make decisions or impose sanctions. Settlement terms reached and agreed to by the parties during the mediation become binding only when and if the parties sign a written settlement agreement.

To mediate could potentially be the resolution I was looking for. The desire to get it all out and move on is what I personally needed. The "liberty and justice for all" thing made me stand up versus lie down.

The actual cost of filing for and meeting with a mediator seemed secondary to the energy I had already put into this case. What became more relevant was what the attorney would charge just for the day – five grand right out of the gate. Hence, our attorney did not attend. According to the opposing party, no one was planning on attending on their end either, seller nor attorney. The seller's attorney sent a letter to my husband and me describing their lack of interest and offered $1,500 in lieu of attending. If I interrupted someone's day and caused a four-hour trip to LA to sit through mediation that could potentially last up to eight hours and then a four-hour return trip, I personally saw this as acceptable. It's the least they could do. I filed and selected the mediator. A date was chosen, a location confirmed, and all those attending were to be identified to each party one week prior to the date of mediation. My list of attendees included my sister Kate, Keith, and our home inspector Dennis. On a separate list, our agent Dick and his broker were invited, but because he was "not interested in tarnishing his record," we left him in his own room. The indescribable position of bringing in the nephew and potentially the aunt into mediation hung over me like a dark cloud. Could I be jeopardizing my husband's career? Either way, the referral fee birthday money was not going to play well for him, nor was his lack of ethical and fiduciary responsibility to us. Let's just say, all cards aside, he could have sat with the opposing party – the seller and seller's attorney.

Entering LA and navigating to Burbank seemed surreal. *Hollywood Squares*, one of Grandma Sally's favorites, was filmed here along with one of my own favorites, *Let's Make a Deal*. And that, I believed, was the game we were going to play. I didn't bring with me a super large purse with everything in it, including a rolling pin or frying pan, but I did bring along a stack of papers eight inches thick, equivalent to the time spent in the house – eight months. The office in which we gathered barely accommodated the conference table, let alone four people, but when the ego of the mediator stepped in, I felt my back up against the wall, and as we all sat, he stood. If the bully in the room was the mediator, then who were the bullies in the other room that felt their time wasn't worth their appearance? Well, let's just say, it wasn't the seller. The listing agent's father, yes, the tenant, came to the mediation, representing his daughter, his employer, and I guess himself, along with the actual seller's attorney. At that moment, I would have thought the mediator, named Clifford Surelacker, an attorney himself, would have canceled the mediation out of unlawful representation of who was supposed to have attended. The $5,000 attorney fee to represent us at this point would have paid for itself. The unfolding of the day labored over pointing fingers. And truly that's how it started.

The mediator indicated three responsible "at fault" parties, and one of those, he noted as he directly pointed his finger, was me. How would I have ever prepared for that? The mediator has already convicted me, completely contrary to the true meaning of "mediator." This brought out my fight-or-flight response, and I really wasn't in the mood to be bullied. When asked what I was here for, I simply said I wanted them to take the house back. A true icebreaker, perhaps that took the mediator off guard, but it conveyed to the entire room that I was not going to take any more of this bullying, and I was not giving up. Eyeing my stack of papers, I think the mediator said, "We may be able to get you a maximum of $2,500, and even that is going to be very difficult, most likely impossible." Impossible was not a word in my creative realm.

Each party at our table was addressed by Clifford the Mediator and asked their reason for attending. Incorrectly, he addressed my sister as Kate and was immediately corrected. She told the mediator he could call her Katlyn. My eyes certainly widened as this statement rolled out of her mouth and across the room. We were off and running and ran right by the $2,500 cap in the first hour. The convoluted story continued to unfold well past the five o'clock hour, and as the minutes added up, so did the dollar bills. The mediator floated in one room and out into the other. He brought in figures which were negotiated and refused. As drawn out as this could possibly be, Clifford benefits as well. Clifford is paid by the hour. We sat through nine hours of mediation, and I was still holding the last card to be played. To gather strength, I thought of one of my favorite quotes by an unknown author, "Speak the truth even though your voice shakes." With a shaky voice, the words slowly escaped my mouth. I stared at Keith from across the table and turned over my final card. "Our agent gave his Uncle Claude (Keith's boss) and his wife Ruth a referral fee for the sale of our home." Exposing that a referral fee was paid to unlicensed agents (Ruth and Claude) put our family in jeopardy of losing Keith's employment. Should we really keep going? The no-arms-length transaction, and reality that the "real seller" did not show, combined with insurance fraud, and on and on and on. It was then and there that I inadvertently pointed my finger back at the mediator.

I really don't know what battle cry summoned their attention, but when the mediator left, he came back with double digits. Could this be a start to my recovery process or the beginning of something even greater?

The parties heading back to the San Diego area were to leave first, and we were to remain in the room. As for our agent and his broker that were held in the small room with no interaction, well, it was a long, drawn-out day for both. But in my eyes, I saved them, and Dick, who clearly knew his mistakes, should have felt a sense of relief. They were pardoned on paper, but the guilt of their negligence can wear on them at another time and place. Our home inspector left the room followed by Keith. As Keith walked ahead, he was approached by the listing agent's father and was told, "If I ever see your face again . . ." The seller's attorney pulled him back, and they left. Shortly thereafter, Kate and I left with the same pile of paperwork. No refractions or reprimands to the listing agent, just a disgusted conviction that money can buy just about anything. Within a week of attending mediation, I pursued the California Bureau of Real Estate and began the formal application of filing a complaint against the entire process. And within the same week, the check from mediation arrived, paid to us by the "actual" seller, confirming my belief that if you don't stand for something, you'll fall for anything.

I fell into a well of my own despair, and by faith, God pulled me out of it. This time, I didn't quit or pull off into a snowbank. Zig Ziglar said, "When obstacles arise, you change your direction to reach your goal; you do not change your decision to get there." And, as Eleanor Roosevelt said, "With the new day comes new strength and new thoughts."

CHAPTER 23

Westward Ho

By the time May arrived, greater triumphs were on the horizon. Kevin was graduating from college back in Wisconsin, and sitting in the auditorium with hundreds of other parents, I felt pure joy. What an incredible day. Even with the brief May snowfall, it was like a fresh start to everyone's future. And in our son's future . . . moving was on the horizon. Moving from the college house he called his Wisconsin home for the past two years; he was now moving forward with a new career and to a new apartment. A U-Haul, a particular baseball cap, and a sense of humor made this move memorable as well as successful. I saw the maturity in my son and felt peace knowing he was starting his life even if it was still 2,000 miles away from ours.

With our son's move complete, hanging out at the lake house with family and friends felt like another extended vacation. Several of my friends would drive out, and we would walk around the lake. An approximate five-mile trek where we hugged the side of the road, which felt like each other. We listened and directed our steps to engage in each other's lives. By the end of each walk, we ached from the mileage, but felt revived. Spiritually refreshed by nature. Hot and sweaty of course from the magnificent sun, always gravitating toward the ray of hope. Barbara and Jackie, I don't know how you did it. Listening to my woes had to sound like a mumbled jumbled mix of crazy stories coming from somewhere out of the Wild Wild West, but you did it, and I am grateful.

By mid-June, five months after I filed, a letter came from the Bureau of Real Estate indicating that they had assigned an investigator to my case. And I think if Chris Farley were still alive, what would have rolled out of his mouth when reading this letter would have been something like, "For the love of God, California, it's about time." Along with, "I'm not a native to the land of fruit and nuts, I'm from Wisconsin." Accent and all. I'm beginning to think that's why the feral cats came around. When I called them, the accent threw them off. And by this time, the family of five was joining me twice a day. Once in the morning and again in early evening. But soon, one by one, they started disappearing. Early one morning,

I opened the patio door and was surprised to see a coyote standing near the pool. At first, I thought someone's dog had jumped our fence, until I had both eyes completely open and noticed it was a coyote. Our neighbor said he had seen one or two previously running up the road in front of our house. I am sad to say, several small dogs and cats had gone missing, perhaps the result of coyotes in the area. A surmising but sad thought, for I loved those cats, and their disappearance left me lonely. And if that morning would have been like previous mornings, I would have opened the door, turned around, and proceeded to make coffee. Luckily for me, I must have had both eyes open that morning, or potentially I could have had a guest for breakfast. Bacon, anyone? Now that would have been an experience. Each morning that followed, I cautiously looked both ways before proceeding outside. Taking in the full panoramic view often meant now looking for coyotes, snakes, large spiders, and scorpions. On occasion, I would see a dead scorpion in the pool and share the experience by calling home to my parents. Our neighbor a street over also mentioned that we should take a black light to our backyard at night. To me, that was not considered a form of entertainment, but they just laughed and carried on. The black light would allow us to see how many scorpions were really out there. But in my opinion, one was already one too many. Line dancing lessons at the Watering Wheel was more up my entertainment alley.

Or simply enjoying the beauty of Norco and the community of horse lovers, riding their horses to wherever they needed to go. To play bingo, shop, or even attend outdoor concerts. The calming effect of the community was delivered through the gentleness of the horses. And on occasion, the bellowing calls from the donkey and roosters. Where did we move to again?

Venturing out for walks as I did was also a great way of staying busy and keeping my mind clear. I had an investigator working on my case, and surely this would resolve my woes. But one day, my woes turned into Wows! An eight-mile walk had me thinking many different things, all unrelated to the house. Especially when I encountered men in orange jumpsuits with power tools grooming the sides of the roads. I recall quickly walking down the middle of the road, hopeful for a quick escape. Needless to say, it was hot, my feet hurt, and I didn't have any water with me. And if I had been near a house with a water fountain, I would have hopped in. But no such luck. Still going uphill, I made it past the orange-suited workers. However, when I turned another corner and was now going down the hill, closer to the golf course, I encountered another crew. By now, my walk had to have been priceless. Trying to keep it all together, my legs felt like rubber, and I felt like I was sun drunk. I wasn't staggering, but perhaps swaying or honestly wobbling, and my Saucony running shoes were smoking hot, and my feet, well, by now, I couldn't tell if I had any. I think they melted into my shoes. By the time I returned home, I ate a half of watermelon and soaked in Epsom salts for at least an hour. Someone needs to keep me entertained; going out on my own accord was proving to be problematic.

Soon Cal would be home from college, and together we could all entertain each other, just like the good old days of apartment living. Inviting friends to come out for a visit, along with day trips to LA and Big Bear, Newport, and so on, created much-needed diversions versus the continual focus on the investigation. And as we celebrated one year in our home, I was beginning to make great strides, at least around our neighborhood. I joined a walking group with three other women, went garage saling with them on the weekends, and found great value in the time we spent together. An artist, animal psychologist, sign maker, and me.

On one of those garage-saling adventures, I had my first Prius experience. The Prius was swift and quiet. And being the passenger, the quietness was like creeping up on a sale, waiting to make the pounce on awesome goods we each didn't need but somehow just had to have. It also occurred to me at that moment that maybe I should drive a Prius. If I am going to continue to investigate, I could sneak up versus announce myself in my big white Suburban. This thought, however, quickly dissipated when I realized I couldn't fit a 4 x 8 sheet of plywood in the back. But on this adventure, my ultimate purchase was a lantern. The homeowner, not sure of what I was talking about, asked me to show her. And as I pointed to the lantern, it just so happened to be attached to the column in their front yard. I think the ladies in my group thought I was totally off my rocker until the woman agreed to sell it to me. You see, I had two of the very same lanterns at home; however, one had recently been taken out of commission. One weekend, Kevin put on his cowboy hat and Wisconsin sweatshirt and pretended to be a California lumberjack while he attempted to cut down the California pepper tree that was leaving a mess in our fountain. He did cut the tree down! Along with one stately looking lantern. This sale was the sale of the century for me. She sold the lantern, and it perfectly replaced our broken one.

On another occasion while gathering to walk, one of the ladies introduced me to a new home warranty company and said I should investigate it. And from there, I was right back into the throes of my "Who-Done-It Mystery" days. According to the new home warranty we signed up for, the refrigerator would be covered. Ironically, it was the same home warranty company that covered the property for the past five years, under the tenant's name. Surprised as I was, so were they when they came to service it. The home warranty company said they wrote out a check for a receipt they received for a new refrigerator. Payable, of course, to the tenants. All of this took place three days before we closed on our house. The slick maneuvers and clever underhandedness left me speechless. A family who worked together to deceive just underestimated the family who moved here from Wisconsin. By now, I had numerous computer search sites and had pulled information from all over on each of the characters involved in this ordeal. I was intrigued that the listing agent studied forensic science and had worked as an investigator at the French store, and in 2015, chose to seek her real estate license. Then, within our transaction period, was pulled over for speeding and did not have car insurance. And somehow the car she was driving was somehow related to the brokerage firm she was working for. This new hire, "listing agent," then proceeded to sell her parents' home as her first home, and lived in it while doing so? Where's the full disclosure? If this is a game of *Jeopardy!*, I will take "What isn't fake in California for $200.00," please. Oh, that's right, this isn't Jeopardy! It's Double Jeopardy! And with Double Jeopardy!, you cannot be charged for the same crime twice. The listing agent became the protected party through mediation, and no refractions could be made against her. Lovely. California is a lovely state to visit, but the people are less than attractive.

CHAPTER 24

Dixie to the Rescue

As time marched on, the fact-finding mission I was on with the California Bureau investigator seemed impossible. My requests were denied, and I was unable to provide the documents they were requiring: a picture of the mother and daughter duo, a copy of the Zillow report, a water bill with the payee's name on it, and validation that the agent lived in the house. If I'm doing all that, what was she doing? I wasn't kidding earlier about the DNA test strips or the camera with zoom lens, for they would have come in handy at this point.

Someone, please rescue me! With a nod of my ponytail and my arms crossed in front of me, my request was somewhat answered.

One Saturday morning in August, Keith, Cal, and I went

on a little adventure to an All-Breed Dog Rescue located in Yucaipa, a city approximately 10 miles east of San Bernardino and about 40 miles from our home in Norco. According to Keith, we were on a "look-only mission," but when we arrived and they let out six little puppies, one little black puppy ran right up to me and put her paws on my thighs, which put my husband's hands into his wallet. And since he was only planning on visiting, he had to go to an ATM and left my son and me with our newest family member, Rachel. She was not the Airedale we were looking for, but she was a sweetheart all the same. Scuffed up with scratches on her tummy and on her nose, she looked weary from what was happening, but she was a fighter. I knew if she could survive this shelter, she was just like her new mother, trying to survive California. The shelter was rat-infested and served what looked like green meat. There were countless dogs looking and barking out for someone to take them home.

Rachel's true mother was found in a field with her litter of puppies by a woman who lived close by. The woman noticed a coyote taking pups away one by one and rescued the remaining family. Cal and I both looked at each other, and without saying a word, we knew she was coming home with us. Perhaps not as Rachel, or even as Milly, but as Dixie. Winn Dixie to be exact. For our family, her little life goes on as in the movie *Because of Winn Dixie*, which is also a name of a grocery store chain in Florida. And here in Yucapia, home to the Stater Brothers grocery chain, this little Dixie would now have two brothers as well. I knew it had to be a Winn in our lives, and we brought her home that very same day. We introduced her to her new surroundings and made several accommodations for her. I asked Keith to cut our laundry door in half and make a Dutch door. This way, her kennel door could remain open and she could have full access to the laundry room/office. I remember closing the half door and walking towards the kitchen when suddenly I heard a noise. Dixie, just six months old, must have taken a running leap and cleared the half door of the laundry room and ran towards me. I knew I had a fighter on my hands. I may have rescued her, but she was already rescuing me.

Dixie was my comfort keeper. She instinctively knew her role far before I ever imagined it. She guarded the house, protected me, and rode shotgun with a paw over my shoulder when we ventured out. She insisted on a bedtime routine and circled the bed around and under before I jumped in. Once I was lying down, she returned to her open kennel in our bedroom.

Maybe a rescue center for dogs is really a rescue center for humans. We took Dixie home that day and provided her with a new family and home, and in return, she provided us with pure joy! And later, a clear understanding that, when removed from your familiar surroundings, it takes time to adapt. Dixie needed time, and so did I. Hindsight of course.

Venturing out on walks as we did in the beginning only took us to the end of our drive. From there, in order to move on, I had to pick her up and carry her. Time eventually favored her ability to continue our walks, but her timid nature called out security over adventure, which was quite relatable to her human. Trust was eroding all around me, much like the rain causing ruts on the horse paths in front of our house. Keen to my surroundings, I too did not favor unsuspecting surprises. I didn't want to live just to the edge of my drive, I wanted to explore new areas and move beyond the silver car, the white Kia, and the pickup truck.

CHAPTER 25

One Hell of a Rodeo

Continually contemplating the direction my life was going, I decided to buy a cowboy hat. Maybe even boots, spurs, and a gun. I could then kick myself in my own butt and shoot for the moon at the same time. Faith always refreshed me in the morning, but by night, darkness and despair crept in. Why is this happening to me? How in the world am I going to jump this next hurdle? How could I possibly accomplish the tasks the investigator assigned to me? Do I cover them with a rug, run around them, or jump over them? I couldn't do any of the above. Past experiences told me that. I had to address the woes and make them wins. Dixie taught me that if you want it bad enough, just jump over the laundry room door. So restless with the lack of support from the Bureau investigator, I continued to search out additional information on my own.

I kept in contact with our California attorney and tried to reach out to the Bureau for further assistance. And when all else failed, I planned another trip to Wisconsin. The lake house rental became my refuge, and the family who owned it my "life preserver." The owner's compassion consoled me, the wine mellowed me, and the pontoon rides that started by the couple picking me up when I was at the end of my rope, or rather at the end of the rental pier, kept me afloat. And just as we went around the lake, the couple circled back to asking Keith to rejoin his former company. Moving forward with my life now meant the possibility of moving back to Wisconsin. An unbelievable series of events, wouldn't you say?

Overwhelmed with relief, but flatlining on excitement, I found myself in a predicament of uncertainty. How is it going to fare with Cal, who was undeniably adapting to California and to college and who was discovering new interests? Now he would be left behind. Am I running in my skates again and not finishing the race? Am I a pawn? I want this nightmare to end, but I am not finished here, I can't just leave. Well, it's not over until the fat lady sings. So I've heard.

Keith now had a new role as the Director of Operations of not just one, but three companies. And ironically, as quickly as he accepted, he was asked to start. My September trip back to Wisconsin was cut short. I returned to California to care for Dixie, and the revolving door of the rental became Keith's home for the next nine months. I was in California, and he was in Wisconsin. Here we go again. September also meant that Cal would be heading back to school, and the remaining parties in Norco would be Dixie and me.

Deciding to take a gun safety test was a no-brainer. Installing a security system – not a problem. Living in Southern California by myself? Now that was going to be interesting. Selling the house and following up with the Bureau were my number one goals. I called the investigator regarding my case, seeing how it was already eight months into the investigation, and asked for an update. I also said that we were putting our house on the market and were moving back to Wisconsin. In hindsight, I wish I hadn't said that. I think the Bureau's investigation stopped right then and there; however, I wasn't quite certain if theirs had ever even started. I offered to drive to San Diego to meet in person to review my case, but she preferred to meet me at our home. Another red flag. This was probably not in my best interest, strictly hers, but I agreed. I guess I was anticipating reviewing everything she had investigated; instead, she wanted to see everything I had. What I produced covered our island from one end to the other. What she brought along were empty hands. Curious as to her position, I asked her what the outcome would be as it stood. And she said, "We'll get her the next time, most offenders are re-offenders." Honestly, I thought someone should have investigated the investigator. A pay-off perhaps? An ulterior motive for waiving the wrongs and making them seem right? Regardless, the Bureau still perceived this as a cold case; however, in my opinion, it was too hot not to see the red cinders or feel the heat. It was pure heat coming from the refrigerator as well, and we replaced it with a new GE Profile unit, priced at $9,000.

Damn it. This made me nosedive into the real estate books I brought home from my sister Kate's house. Could this be real estate protocol? Protect the agents and not the citizens? Somehow, I thought the Bureau was a program funded by the state, paid by the taxpayers of the state. Damn it. This is a disaster. After the investigator left, I went right to work and hired my own private investigator to help me out. At this point, what did I have to lose? My relationship with my California friend Ruth? It felt like she only called to take my pulse. I honestly couldn't tell if she called to see what I was up to, or if she felt a sense of responsibility for the way the home transaction went. Or maybe she wanted to keep an eye or an ear out for her nephew, Dick – who knows. Early on in our relationship, she told me she liked to hang out with people she could learn from. For example, her mother-in-law, about whom she said, "She knows exactly how to ask questions in a way that is unassuming, so no one knows that she is digging." Wow, now that was an interesting comment shared by someone whom I had just met. And, when she was in Wisconsin, I do recall her asking me, "What is Keith doing at the company?" What???? I didn't know the answer to that question. I had just thawed out from the winter, the twinkling lights at the store, and the move.

But if crazy is what it takes, I'm in. We had been in California for one year and five months, and I wanted to make the best of the time we had left. It was October, and with Keith living in Wisconsin, we decided it would be fun to throw a party the next time he flew back. We never had a housewarming, so a going-away party suited us well. Trying to keep whatever ties we made with friends, co-workers, and neighbors, I thought having a Halloween party would be perfect. A weekend where Keith would fly back to California and we could have everyone over to say goodbye sounded great. Invitations went out, and decorations were hung, and I searched for a costume. Who would I want to be? I shopped for a costume for Dixie and lassoed a cowboy hat with red braids, much too cute to pass up. As for myself, frankly, our staircase called for a *Gone with the Wind* costume, but I settled for *Breakfast at Tiffany's* and entertained in a long black dress, tiara, sunglasses, and gloves. Keith, on the other hand, was a cowboy. And from there, we had characters from *The Wizard of Oz*, hippies from the '60s, some smarty-pants, a pink flamingo, a zoologist, scary mommy, and others. The smarty-pants couple had my vote for the best costume. Simple, sweet, and clever. Jell-O shots, great food and company, and a flaming pumpkin topped off the evening. I felt for the first time that evening like a superhero conquering my fears of what I felt was conquering me, or was I still hiding behind the shades of my sunglasses? I showcased our home for what it became and made good out of the bad. I invited Ruth and her husband Claude, his brother Walter, and his wife, Ramona, along with others from Keith's work and neighbors.

But perhaps my costume only fooled me, for it didn't get any better as time progressed at the house. The same car still parked outside our house, and an edginess still lingered. Keith flew back to Wisconsin, and I stared at the real estate sign I had put in our yard. I was determined to stay the course until it sold. However, within a month, I re-evaluated the "for sale by owner" and called Kate to list our home. She replied that she would not be the best agent, for she was not in our marketplace, and though in the same state, Northern and Southern California are not the same. I contacted a Century21 office in our town, and that interview enlightened my day. She brought with her a preliminary title search, as she called it, indicating that we purchased the home in 2010. Seriously, I just about fell off my counter stool. I told her we purchased the home in 2015. Puzzled now as well, she showed me the document and said we should make an inquiry to the title company. Another inquiry? Frankly, I was ready to make an anonymous phone call to the

FBI. Ironically, the person I needed to contact had the same last name as the neighbor who didn't want anything to do with us. 2010 was the year that home was short-sold to the employer, who then allowed the employee, AKA original owners, to continue to live there. The original owners should have been on the title for 2010, not us. Rattled now by the title error, I couldn't commit to this firm or any firm until I got this corrected.

Anyway, as the day ended, Angela Lansbury, AKA Jessica Fletcher, AKA me, went back to work. Amateur detective, yes; writer, no. That was the furthest thing from my mind. However, I began to see that I needed to keep all the paperwork straight. By now, I had a 10-inch stack of paperwork. Copies of contracts, photocopies of documents, mediation information, prior home sale activity, and so on, and now, incorrect title information. I found myself buying cigarettes and would often sit on our patio and chain-smoke. The mornings still consisted of my 7:00 a.m. phone call, followed by a podcast, a walk, and by lunchtime, two or three cigarettes. By four o'clock, which would have been six Wisconsin time, I was calling Keith and asking for a divorce. He would agree to it, so I would hang up, drive through the In-N-Out Burger, eat a burger, sip my vanilla shake, and swallow my woes. Return to the patio, have one or two more cigarettes, and then by dusk, I would sit in the house with Dixie and watch TV. I became a Netflix junkie. I started binge-watching some of Cal's favorite shows and would often catch up to where he left off, and then pass him up. This always provoked an interesting phone call, beginning with, "Mom, what are you doing?" Of course, I followed up with, "Not much, why do you ask?" Funny how family dynamics change a bit, isn't it? But it was time to start paying more attention to finding a realtor than to watching all the episodes of *Breaking Bad* (although that did give me a whole new thought process to seeing houses tarped for termites). We decided to continue our interviewing process.

Focused on the desired result of selling the house, I reached out to one of my friends from the Ladies of the Round Table in WI to inquire about her sister's friend, who was a realtor in Southern California. And as impossible as it sounds, the woman who was recommended to us worked for the same brokerage firm as Dick, who sold us our home. Clearly, this was not meant to be, and our search continued. I received a referral from my sister, and this superseded my husband's five interviews along with mine as well. I met with the referred listing agent, and we chatted for about 30 minutes at my kitchen table. We discussed professional photography, access to the house, a broker's open, and open houses, etc. With a professional agent handling our house sale, I decided to look for a part-time job. Something other than TV to entertain me. I spent more time now working part-time at a retail store as seasonal help. I shopped for online orders and pushed a six-foot cart (after removing one of the bins so I could see). Classic.

CHAPTER 26

Karaoke at the Old Saloon

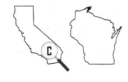

It was now late November, and with the house as tidy as it could possibly be on the inside, I turned my magic outward and focused on painting the exterior trim, shutters, entranceway, and front door. It looked incredible, if I must say so myself. The 26-foot ladder paid for itself over and over, and my calves and leg muscles felt the burn. I personally still felt like I could power through anything, but what I couldn't provide to the investigator kept me struggling. Keith knew what I needed to get my mind off the house and sent six young men to the house for a visit. Yes, the Suburban made an airport run and picked up six young men, including my son Kevin and five of his Wisconsin friends; it was like winning the lottery. Kevin, Derek, Jake, Aaron, Grayson, and Ben all spent a long weekend in Norco, entertaining me, probably more than they knew, but all enjoying themselves California-style. They included "Mom" in much of everything they did, including a night at the Saddle-Sore Saloon, which was worth a thousand evenings of entertainment. Cal also joined us, creating what someone at the bar thought was a mom bringing in a soccer team. I explained that these were all my kids and called out for a round of hurricane shots and karaoke for everyone! Belting the latest and greatest tunes each could carry, we laughed, roared, and drank until our courage took the stage. A night of *America's Got Talent* erupted into a stage, mic, and lights phenomenon. If you showed up, you got up and sang the tune of your choice. I chose "Tennessee Whiskey," but it didn't choose me. Not a great fit and not a note I could carry. Empty-handed in the singing department, I don't even know how I held the microphone. The song started without me, and I had to quickly catch up. Not as smooth as Tennessee whiskey, and less sweet than strawberry wine, I still made it through to the end. The song is reminiscent of California. I heard it in our family room for the first time when at the 49th Annual Country Music Awards in 2015. Chris Stapleton and Justin Timberlake captured my turbulent year. "Tennessee Whiskey" was followed by "Drink You Away." I had never really consumed a lot of alcohol on a continual basis until I lived in California. Its effect gave me a double set of puffy cheeks and a reason for not getting up in the morning, if you catch my drift. With the dry heat, and the incredible drought California was experiencing, the thought of lighting more matches seemed incredibly more dangerous, so I quit the smoking stint and red-wined my way through the rest of my stay.

That same weekend the kids came to visit, the Santa Ana winds picked up. Fifty-mile-per-hour winds drove through our backyard, pulling up one of our pepper trees, which then landed on the house to the right of us. If delivering Christmas cookies wasn't well received, delivering the news that our tree fell on their house was going to bring on all kinds of excitement. The sight of the shagbark pepper tree nestled against their house and clay shingled roof was a jaw-dropper for me. I had to be the bearer of bad news. This time standing at their red front door knocking, I had very little words or expression. Just like on the TV series, *Dragnet*, I was delivering just the facts. I knocked several times, the wife answered in her PJ's, and I delivered the message. One of our trees was uprooted last night and fell on the side of your house. Boom! Done! I then felt the stare-down. I asked her to look at the tree, and she followed me. She observed the tree and said her husband would handle it. I walked back to her front door with her, thinking I would talk to the husband, but as she crossed the threshold of the doorway, she turned and pointed to the deadlocks. She told me she had five dead bolts and closed the door.

Wow, what was that all about? Five dead bolts? I thought to myself, *Do I need more? Where in the world am I?* Well, for starters, I'm roughly three blocks away from a recently discovered crack house. I'm on a street where a friendly-looking neighbor, a middle-aged doctor, died from what could have been a concoction of the wrong medications. I'm being followed by a woman in a white Kia and watched by a woman in a silver car daily in front of my house. If I've picked up any friends, paranoia was not one of them. These were the facts; call me Sgt. Joe Friday if you want, or call me any other day of the week, for I am reporting "just the facts, ma'am." I called a tree trimming company, and they removed the tree and took the logs and branches as if nothing ever happened. And it appeared that nothing ever did happen. The neighbor never called or inquired. Something didn't sit well, even with the tree removed.

Ironically, if you recall, our neighbor's last name matched the last name of the person who was responsible for correcting our title information. What an incredible coincidence! And why that tree, on that house, when we have several trees all over our yard? Perhaps a little help from above? Meaning, keep your friends close and your neighbors closer? The continual encounters left me pondering my next move. I took the kids back to the airport and turned the calendar to December.

With lots of retail holiday hours, work was a pure distraction for me. The fa la la la's and ha ha ha's kept me entertained each shift I worked. I thought of myself as Santa's little helper, fulfilling orders by gathering items off the shelves, putting them in my cart, and shipping them out to customers. Quite an experienced shopper myself, I thought it would be a breeze. But what I didn't expect was that the list was not written on paper, it was on a handheld device that some called a blue bird, however, at the end of each shift, I just wanted to give it the bird. It was easier for me to pick up a paintbrush than carry around a handheld computer.

Electronics were not my thing. And this became quite evident one day while I was busy putting merchandise in boxes, taping them shut, and adding shipping labels. My little electronic device, once complete, was now missing its back. Oh, where or where did it go? It was nowhere to be found, however, I just carried on with my shift. It fit well into the charging station, and the next day, when someone else grabbed it, that person was thrilled that it fit in his pocket. Moving on, I was put at the registers where a "Ding Ding" ring of a bell did not mean an angel got its wings. It simply indicated that another lucky consumer was issued a credit card. For a minute there, I was bell-happy. I hit the button that rang the bell even before the register indicated an approval of credit. However, it stopped the moment the individual was declined. It then became the saddest form of an employment request ever, and my heart sank. Here is where commercialism won out, and I was indebted to helping others acquire debt. With continued shifts at the register, I focused on consumer awareness. I saw repeat shoppers and repeat return pros. I saw customers eager to have a conversation while checking out, while others didn't want to say a word. One lady came in and was angered to learn that the hanger which indicated extra large did not match the item of clothing. The actual clothing was medium. At my register, I called for department assistance, and a larger size was not available. I offered to call another store, and she started to cry. She decided to keep the current size, and as she checked out with additional items she shopped for that day, she still seemed to be missing something, and I said as much to her. She looked surprised when I said she was missing something: a hug. I walked around the counter, gave this woman a hug, and wished her a very Merry Christmas. "Happy Holidays" is pure commercialism, and I wanted no part of that. Shocked, she stood back, and her tears rolled into a smile. Those were the moments I was missing, and perhaps she was too. She continued to make her way back to the store in the weeks to come, and I believe it was because she found so much more than what was on her list. Fill people's hearts by having compassion, it's priceless.

It is easy at Halloween to put on a costume and be whoever you want to be, but at Christmastime, wouldn't it be great if everyone could put on a smile and wear a piece of their heart on their sleeve? We all have a heart, correct? Or at least something that resembles one? Moments like these and others made this little job less entertaining and more meaningful than I ever would have imagined.

I had a shift where a woman walked into the men's department and needed a tie for her husband. My manager called me while I was working the register and asked if I could help her. She told me she needed more than a tie, but someone to tie it as well. Capable of assisting, I was relieved at the registers and met the woman in the men's department. The woman had already selected the tie and handed it to me. I placed the tie around her neck and tied a Double Windsor. As I was standing directly in front of this stranger, she told me it was for her husband, who needed to wear a tie to her father's funeral that afternoon. She went on to say her husband worked in construction all his life and never wore a tie. And she had no idea what to do. I realized then that we weren't complete strangers. We were really "family," in this big crazy world, and if we could just treat others the way we would like to be treated, we would all be living the good life.

I thank my younger brother Ely for allowing me to help this woman. Earlier on, when my kids were gearing up for dances, Ely gave Kevin a cardboard instruction tie guide that hung on Kevin's bulletin board for years. I personally admired the Double Windsor, the classiest look, and I practiced it each time the kids had a special occasion. That's not entertainment or employment, that's compassion. Cynicism can only last so long.

CHAPTER 27

AD Troubles

If ADT stands for American District Telegraph, then my interpretation allows it to stand for Ally Diedrick Troubles. Just by tap, tap, tapping away on my electronic devices, the more I searched, the more I discovered, and the more troubling this whole ordeal had become. What I really needed was a new attorney and an ADT security system. A sense of security by now would be awesome. But unfortunately, when I had the ADT installed, instead of feeling secure, I would lie in bed at night, waiting for the alarm system to go off. Perhaps it was the salesman's approach, telling me his uncle and aunt were murdered a day before their system was installed, by the son, who was released from prison a day before his stated release date. The ADT was installed a day too late. Wow, what a sales pitch. I bought it and had it installed the same day.

Next on my list, a new attorney and a buyer for our home. It was that simple. The house was impeccable, fresh, clean, and beautiful. Basically, I occupied the house as a full-time decorator, housekeeper, and gardener. What more could one ask for? On the other hand, I wanted something for myself before we sold. I wanted all the humanly wrongs made right. Peace, transparency, and my life back. By reaching out to a Wisconsin friend who was also an attorney, I received a referral for an attorney roughly 30 miles away. I called that very day and scheduled an appointment. The receptionist told me I would have a 30-minute consultation, for a fee of course. Then the practice would determine if they would take the case. Already familiar with the area, I felt at ease with the directions and looked forward to the visit.

Meanwhile, back at the ranch, our agent Martha informed me that we had two showings scheduled. A couple from the LA area and a couple from Riverside. At last, everything seemed to be picking up momentum. I could feel the energy and warmth from the sun again and was less distracted. I started to wake up feeling refreshed. My energy level picked up, and so did the pace of my stride. I started walking, mid-morning power walks and late afternoon strolls.

One morning, I found myself crossing our street and

following the curb down to the stop sign versus walking on the path directly in front of our house. It was then that I noticed a small car turning up our street. As it approached me, I noticed the driver had on the strangest outfit. It was hot, but the small-framed woman had on a gray, hooded sweatshirt with the hood pulled tightly around her face, framing out her dark sunglasses and blank expression. It was the strangest look I have seen thus far in California. I have seen UGGs worn in 60-degree temps with winter coats, mittens, and hats, but this took the cake. Could I rationalize this scenario? Our street only had houses on one side of the street. A newly divorced couple, a retired couple, our house, the title company name association neighbor, the doctor who died, the family with kids, and a recent couple who just moved in who owned a pool company. So, this obviously stuck with me all day and into the evening. Why I crossed the street that morning and walked on the opposite side of the road, making it so easy to identify the woman driving the car, stumped me. Very few cars traveled on our street. I must try harder at sidestepping the negative and think positive, stay motivated, and move on and avoid the manure.

What could possibly be worse? Well, I made one last attempt at connecting with Ruth, thinking I could ask for one simple favor of her. The call was easy to make, but apparently answering was difficult for her. We chatted a bit, and then I asked her for a huge favor. I asked her to ask her nephew Dick one question. Did he ever look on Zillow in regards to our home? I knew it would be a long shot since he never looked on the MLS, but it was worth a try. If he did, could he recall the section noted "What I Love About the Home" and the statement made about a $90,000 kitchen remodel? Her reply to me was, "Yes, I will ask." That moment, I felt unbelievable JOY. But as quickly as it came, it left. She later texted and said it was too late in the evening to ask him and she was too busy during the day. However, she texted again and asked if we would be getting together soon for lunch. Thinking about how I would respond, I decided I needed fresh air and a diversion. I was going to play Bingo that evening, and I was prepared to scream the loudest Bingo ever. And if I was lucky enough to win, I would like my prize to be a buyer for our house and a get-out-of-California-free card. But wait, that's another game.

I contemplated staying home that evening, seeing how everyone I invited was either too busy or not feeling well. My neighbor who lost her husband was one I was hopeful would join me, but I really wasn't quite sure what role she played. Was she a double agent? Friend to the listing agent perhaps? Regardless, I was far beyond creating another twist to this story. I was already riding on the edge. I decided the entertainment alone was worth it and got ready for a night of Bingo. I opened the garage door, backed out, and headed down our street towards the stop sign. As I turned right and continued towards the Bingo hall, I saw a vehicle parked on the side of the road, backed in to face oncoming traffic. It totally unnerved me, and I turned at the next street to head back home. The unsuspecting decorator turns detective. Truly this started to irritate me because it made me feel more suspicious. But who was left in this state I could trust? It just had to be coincidence, right? I called Keith in Wisconsin, and he affirmed that I was just being overly cautious and avoided the word "paranoid." That would have cost him another divorce discussion. Honestly, at this point, I couldn't have been any more cognizant of my surroundings.

And within my surroundings, how much more $h?t could happen? Ruth ended up saying she was too busy to call her nephew and couldn't help me. The word "friend" fell quickly into horse manure, and we were now acquaintances, if that. It was the last straw in my bale. With so many occasions ending badly, my only recourse was to infer she had greater problems than me, and from what you could tell, I had plenty, but she must have had more. The second to last straw ended just as badly. I was invited to the birthday party of her one-year-old grandson. I accepted and arrived early. I said hello to her husband, and he motioned to where Ruth was standing. I walked over to her, and she mentioned that she was going to grab a bowl of chili and we could sit and chat. As that happened, her sister-in-law, Mable, approached our table, who was the mother-in-law to

Dick, who sold us the house. She acted like we had never met before, but soon she knew who I was and commented "Oh, you're the one." She then immediately made her way to the back pool area. Ruth then got up from the table and said, "I'm going to join my family." Now sitting at the table by myself, I wanted to stand up and give the entire family a red card. A soccer penalty card pulling everyone out of the game. What the hell is going on here!? Hell, I gave myself a red card for showing up, and I got up and left. I never received a thank-you note for the gift I gave, but I did, however, consider writing my own thank-you note(s). And it would be a two-parter, something like this: Thank you to the National Company that brought us out to California. And then I would highlight their own words, surmising their family as being passionate and united as well as committed to learning from one another. Of course, this scenario would define why I became a stockholder. I believed their statement and balance sheet for that matter, and now would ask them to believe mine. As a stockholder and wife to your recent hire, I object to the use of nepotism. And for this reason alone, the opportunity for my family to relocate concluded with a real estate transaction that ended poorly and, within two short years, a resignation and legal U-turn back to Wisconsin. The family and leader at the location in Orange, California, involved themselves in our real estate transaction, which produced a financial reward aiding a sale, yet remained mute when aiding the new hire when assistance was asked for. My second thank-you is to Ruth and Claude, for undeniably allowing me to see the writing on the wall and incredible story to be written. Our short stay in California produced a long story of disbelief. I didn't move in faith, but faith brought me back, and I am grateful.

CHAPTER 28

Can You Win by Losing?

Yes, I lost at Bingo that night, but won at following through on my scheduled appointment with the attorney. I drove the 30 minutes or so to an area which was now very familiar from prior shopping and sightseeing visits. I felt very calm and prepared. I parked on the opposite side of the street and walked towards the office building. I opened the door and was overwhelmed by the reception area. Incredible arrangements of fresh flowers and planters of white lilies surrounded the desk. As I walked forward, I saw more flowers and a woman behind the desk, perhaps the receptionist, holding a tissue to her face and wiping tears from her eyes. In a soft voice, she asked, "Can I help you?" "Yes," I said and introduced myself. I told her I was here to see John McLean, and then silence followed. With great pain and quivering lips, she said he passed away last week. She gathered more courage and told me he was in a bicycle accident in the mountains. I let her do all the talking, and she shared his story.

He was 65, an avid biker, and was getting ready to retire. My heart hurt for his office family, for I could feel the love they had for him. I wondered why they didn't call me to reschedule, so I asked the question. The woman replied in a more business-like manner and told me they were prepared to continue and brought in another attorney with whom I could meet. At that moment, I almost forgot what I came for. Oh, that's right, a simple consultation, and that couldn't have been canceled? The woman behind the desk got up and went to the office down the hall and returned with another woman. Watery eyes and a painful smile suggested she was also mourning the loss of her co-worker, and with that aura, my heart sank. A moment of gathering my own thoughts felt like an hour. When motioned to follow her, I felt startled. Slow to respond, I picked up my tote of papers and followed her into a conference room. We sat across from each other, and in the middle of the table sat a box of tissues. Tears were in her eyes and quickly began to form in mine. I felt my problems dissolving from her tears. I grabbed a tissue and couldn't move beyond that. I felt heaviness in my heart, and it weighed me down. I could barely move my arms, much less pick up the tote with all my investigative finds.

Perhaps I was supposed to listen to her, and at that moment, she began without hesitation.

She said the entire office was devastated beyond belief, and she was brought into the office to assist during the bereavement and to continue with the caseloads. With a yellow legal pad and pen, she asked me to state the reason for the consultation. I felt like I was already talking to someone who was a thousand miles away. Trying to stay focused was an immediate fail; I was already derailed. I studied the outline I prepared, rehearsed, and re-rehearsed and strictly went off that. The crucial event of the short sale, the no-arms-length transaction, the mortgage fraud, the listing agent being the daughter to the original owners. The lack of full disclosure, original owners acting as tenants, insurance fraud, the mediation mishap, the bullying, the recent title search, and lastly the concern that someone was following me were all the reasons for my consultation. I was exhausted.

A 30-minute consult turned into an hour and a half. And at the very end, she apologized and said, "What happened?" I believe she entered the room with me but never heard a word I said. Desperately wanting to cry myself at this point, I said to her, "Is there anything I can do for you?" Lost for words, her blank stare through her bloodshot eyes said it all. She picked up her yellow legal pad and pen, pushed her chair back, and stood up. I gathered my things and followed her back to the reception area where I wrote out a check and left. Feeling sorrow for the office, and hopeless for myself, I slowly walked to the door and gently closed it behind me. Somberly, I headed for the exit of the building. As I neared the street, I looked both ways and proceeded to cross. I sighed and stepped slowly; life is too short for all this bullshit.

And as I began to cross, I looked back to my left, and in the alley of the attorney's office was a white SUV and a blonde-haired woman with sunglasses on standing next to it. What in the hell is happening? How in the world did my life end up like this? I had pondered this question since my move, and as time went on, it only intensified. I called my sister Kate immediately after getting into the car, and we chatted all the way home. Even though she lives five hours away, and literally eight to nine with traffic, it was still a comfort to me knowing that she was in the same state.

By now you must be wondering why I wasn't packing my bags and leaving the state? My reason for staying was backed up by my son's reason for staying. He was now enjoying his new life, and I wasn't going to shift his life to accommodate mine. We already went down that road when we left Wisconsin. What I really needed to do was focus on selling our house. I honestly didn't feel there was anything else I could do at that point. My case seemed fruitless, and I became a California nut.

The following morning, it was the usual 7:00 a.m. call to Kate, and she too agreed that life is too short. "Let it go," she said. I was fighting the principle of the matter. And if losing means I tried, could it feel better than quitting?

The consensus was I should concentrate on selling the house and move back to Wisconsin. My husband agreed. He also said he would fly out so we could spend a long weekend together. And within the same phone conversation insisted that we both return to Wisconsin. I believe the last statement fell onto deaf ears. I didn't want to leave my son, nor my house. My choices were counterintuitive to my "don't quit" principle. Our son was happy at school, and our home was our biggest investment. I was committed to staying with it until the end.

That weekend when my husband flew in, his 11:00 p.m. arrival was pushed back until midnight or a little after. Dixie and I hopped in the car, opened the garage door, and did our usual "Y" turn to exit the drive. At the end of the drive, I looked both ways before turning onto our street, and to my left, parked right at the edge of our drive, looked liked our neighbor's black Mercedes. The neighbor whom we never communicated with. This was interesting to say the least, and luckily for me, Dixie and I were heading to the airport to pick up and not drop off. Someone needed to see what I was seeing. The headlights on my Suburban highlighted what was literally in front of me. Yes, a black Mercedes. But was it truly my neighbor's? And was my neighbor parked in front of my house at midnight? *Breaking Bad* flashed before my eyes, and I wondered if someone was selling drugs? The tinted windows were beginning to feel like unfair play. I was just happy I didn't back out of our drive and accidently hit this car. Who would have suspected a car there in the first place at midnight? Should I have stopped my car, hopped out, and knocked on the window? Perhaps it was just someone parking and stretching before getting onto the 91? Yes, this was the first time I saw a car parked on the street at the end of our driveway at midnight. But it was also the first night that I went out at midnight. By the time I picked up my husband and returned home, the car had left.

That weekend, we were quite fortunate to have two showings. We already had an open house and a broker's open. And those experiences alone left in me left field. On the first day, two women did our open house, and I felt very comfortable and excited. On the second day, our agent was going to hold it open, and it was raining. Our agent called an hour before the start time and said she would like to cancel. I was puzzled by the consideration to cancel because of rain, and I asked her to hold it open anyway. Surprising to me, but apparently common practice in California, when it rains, the roads get slippery and people stay home. I was persuasive, however, and said the neighbor up the street who was selling was also having an open house, and I think we should proceed. I returned home that day after the open house to find a basket from my first-floor guest room now at my front door, filled with blue booties. And in the kitchen, a teapot which was under the cooktop filled with apple cider. Purely observant, and thoroughly interesting to me, nonetheless. I wasn't sure if I was being overly sensitive or incredibly amazed at how quickly home ownership changes simply by signing a listing contract with a firm. The broker's open also proved to be interesting and brought our neighbor, whose husband had passed. She drove down and parked in the driveway when literally she lived just two houses away. Overly cautious or extremely sensitive, I was cognizant of my surroundings.

Our listing contract requested that all showings include a two-hour notice so I could arrange to take Dixie to the park or have someone care for her if I was working. I also had to ensure that the lockbox would be set outside near the front door. Our agent was to also identify the agent showing the property as well as the potential buyers. A sense of security, but it also allowed me to extend my hospitality as a homeowner, and I popped popcorn and filled small bags for our buyers, along with an arrangement of chilled water bottles and our home binder. The binder came complete with appliance warranties, work performed on the property, age of mechanicals, and community information. Perhaps it was over-the-top to some, but not to me. That weekend, we didn't receive any offers, but with my husband here until Tuesday, all seemed to be A-OK. When Monday morning arrived, so did the mysterious silver car. This time, the woman appeared to stretch as she placed her hand on the trunk and lifted each leg. I asked my husband to go out and check it out for himself. Not her stretching, of course, but the fact that I wasn't stretching my story. He walked across the street and said, "My wife says you park here every morning. Her response was, "Are you still the owners of the white Suburban?" And though my husband answered yes, he also concluded that he had a wife who had been telling him the truth. But, she went on to say, she parked here before getting on the 91. Interesting, for her story had changed. What happened to the day care? The following day, my spouse returned to Wisconsin, alone.

As showings continued, our agent called and said a woman would be showing our home at noon. However, at 10:00 a.m., a man walked into our home with clients in tow. Not quite sure of the protocol, I packed up Dixie, asked the agent to move his Porsche out of the middle of our driveway, and left. I called our agent. She wasn't quite sure what happened and apologized for the inconvenience. I wondered how many more times that might have happened if I had left the lockbox outside? I kept it in the house until I had a showing. However, on that morning, I put it out early so I didn't forget. If I wasn't prepared for the showing at noon, I don't know if I would have remained cool about the misunderstanding.

But as time moved on, things were looking up and more showings were scheduled. Perhaps the best compliment of all came from a father that attended his son and daughter-in-law's second showing. I happened to be walking Dixie that day instead of taking her to the dog park, and I noticed garbage on the road a few yards from our house. I picked it up, and the gentleman asked if I lived in the neighborhood. I said, "Yes, I own the home you just looked at." He said it was the cleanest house in Norco!

Two weeks later, I was in the same routine. Picking up my husband from the airport and looking forward to spending Easter with our son Cal. We had several more showings scheduled, including a couple coming from LA. The agent brought the buyers in, and they loved it. An offer was written, and we accepted. We were beginning to see the end to this whole ordeal. Or so we thought. A week later, we received a call, and the buyers wanted to come back through the house. Interestingly, it wasn't to reconsider their offer, but to add to it. They wanted to purchase items in our home, and the list was extensive and grew to thousands of dollars. Seven thousand, to be exact. And as promised, the following week, they returned with cash in hand. The couple arrived much later than anticipated, and each looked like they came from separate events. He looked like he just came from a basketball game he played in, and she looked like she just left a fashion show – beautifully dressed and polished. On the other hand, my husband and I had on matching outfits, it seemed, for they both commented on our attire. "How cute, you're dressed alike." Were we? I guess if blue jeans and a buttoned-down shirt qualified us? But in my mind, were they checking us out? Stopping by and checking out the house again without their agent? What would be the purpose of wanting to buy Western-looking furniture when their style appeared to be contemporary? The decorator in me was surprised at that indeed. Interesting, isn't it? We welcomed them in, and while sitting in the family room, the husband began to lay out hundreds of hundred-dollar bills on our coffee table for the Western-style furniture they wished to buy. Seven thousand, to be exact. It was like a *furniture deal was going down*. By now, nothing surprised me. Once our agent heard they purchased thousands of dollars of furniture, she told us her husband, also a police officer in LA, knows that some officers who confiscate guns also resell them on the streets for cash. What? Is this gun money? Yes, the buyer from LA was a police officer, but this was the furthest thing from my mind. No way!

The consideration that this was gun money was only second to drug money. This, in fact, could have been a drug house for all I know. The original kitchen sink certainly could have screamed that! Pitted beyond belief by human force! Anyway, the closer we got to selling, the happier I became. But as the contract dates were closing in, we were no more secure that the house was going to close. A delay in securing the loan surpassed the finance contingency, and the contract/offer expired for our LA couple. This brought me back to the furniture they purchased. How do you pay cash for furniture and not secure financing for the home you intend to buy? Or, was the furniture purchased as the opportunity to keep an eye on us? Events like this fueled my imagination and continual apprehension. Why was this all happening? Where did this screenplay come from? Where's my script? Better yet, what does the ending look like, let's skip right to that! I never really started my new life, for each day was a burden of trying to figure out all the obstacles and the hurdles I had to jump the day before. I figure when "hell freezes over," I will have a better understanding of what just happened. Or perhaps when the movie comes out, I will be able to sit back, eat popcorn, and be entertained.

And then . . . more $h?t happened; and yes, this was my first consideration for the title of this book. Not only did our deal fall through with the LA couple, but we experienced a lovely encounter one evening while dining out. Stranger than fiction, as my friend Ella would say. Finally familiar with the community, I took a co-worker's recommendation and suggested to my husband that we have dinner at a little diner in Corona. That evening was iconic. I remember the two of us having a minor argument, and I got up from my table and moved to another. I told the waiter that he could give the bill to the man that I was originally sitting with, but I would be dining alone. My husband at one table, and I at another. The only other couple in the restaurant had to be in their 80s, so I tried not to make a big scene. However, apparently someone else was in there that I hadn't noticed . . . As my husband paid the check, we resumed our partnership and walked out into the parking lot where we both noticed a Prius with the driver's door open. As we walked past the vehicle, we saw a man sitting in the driver's seat with a camera watching the restaurant. We got into our car before staring at each other in bewilderment. Keith then asked, "Who do you suppose he was watching?" OMG what the hell is happening here?

Well, it was more of what was not happening. With the first deal that fell through, our realtor saved the day and announced the other buyer was still interested – the Riverside County buyer. The buyer whose father-in-law said we had the cleanest house in Norco. The offer was written, and we accepted. The new closing date would take us through mid-May. Ample time to have the first buyers come and get their furniture. In the meantime, my saving grace through all of this was Dixie, my trusty companion. She honestly had brought me so much joy in this crazy state I moved into. She was my diversion.

Ally-Dixie ventures to the dog park were eventful, for she sat on the park bench with me probably wondering why I wasn't mingling with the other humans, when in fact I took her so she could play with other dogs. Our co-mingling ventures to the park were frequent, and the results for the most part the same.

By now, my husband had already had his mind set that we were moving before the house closed. He arranged for the movers to pack everything up again, and within a day or two, the large semi appeared in front of our home. Here we go again. All the furniture, with exception of what the first buyers purchased and what was saved for Cal, was loaded. Boxes upon boxes exited the house. And an emptiness and feeling of uncertainty echoed throughout. My husband said he had plans during his stay to deliver Cal's furniture to his frat house. So, the next morning, in a calm and thoughtful manner while sipping coffee, he said he would be picking up a U-Haul trailer. Sounds good to me. By early afternoon, he returned with the U-Haul and said we would be loading it and leaving within four hours. Close to rush-hour traffic, nonetheless, but in Southern California, it's all rush-hour traffic. My husband then said, "You're leaving California tonight as well."

I was standing in the kitchen when these words traveled across the room and hit me like a ton of bricks. It was like the bottom just fell out of my coffee cup, and instead of jumping up and down, it just burned and immobilized me. Steaming from the frustration of another person calling the shots left me unresponsive and silent. I was in total opposition of leaving Cal behind along with our biggest investment still on the market.

I didn't know what to say. Totally frustrated by the house that literally consumed me, the lack of support from the Bureau that left me helpless, and "the husband" calling the shots and disrupting my life made me want to throw something at him! But then, if I did throw something, I would have to clean it up. So, I threw words back instead. "You didn't share in the investigation of the house, you never wanted to go to mediation, and you don't care if the house closes or not, and you're willing to leave our son here?" Silence filled the room. Dazed and confused, I left for the donut shop. I picked up donuts and dropped them off to my recently departed place of business for my co-workers to enjoy and said goodbye. I knew I wasn't going to win this battle with my husband, and I had no alternative options.

We loaded the U-Haul and the white Suburban and packed it the same way it came out. Capacity of eight, and now just enough room for me, my husband, and Dixie. We arrived this time at Cal's home at 7:00 p.m. and unloaded everything he asked for, plus additional treasures. We said our goodbyes, and at approximately 7:30 p.m., headed back to return the U-Haul. From there, we did a quick drive through Chick-fil-A, stopped back at the house because I had left Dixie's medicine in the refrigerator, and jumped back onto the freeway around 9:30 p.m. Ironically, an hour later, my neighbor, the wife of the deceased doctor, called me on my cell phone and said, "I see you are heading home." Please excuse the crazy, but what was going through my mind was "Are you tracking me?" We chatted briefly and hung up. This time, the weather forecast within the cabin didn't call for a chance of rain, I think a tornado was about to hit. I was speechless. Totally frustrated, I could have ripped the muffler off my Suburban, for the roar of leaving would have made a stronger statement versus the quiet departure late in the evening.

My heart couldn't keep up with my emotions. Seat-belted in, this roller-coaster ride took the highs to a brand-new low. Driving through Vegas and into the mountains seemed to have created a time lapse. Was it the sun coming up, or was I oblivious to a full moon? NO, it was the bright light that lit up the dashboard indicating that the vehicle was low on fuel, basically telling the driver, "Hey, buddy, you forgot to fill up!" That was it for me; too close for comfort, no room to vent, I sounded off my first words of the trip, "If we have run out of gas, I am filing for a divorce." The miles to empty on the dashboard stopped at three, and that seemed like 15 miles ago. We had driven to San Diego and back with a trailer, yet the driver must have thought we were in a smart car and we didn't require additional fuel. These were the days that gave me gray hair and PRBF – permanent resting bitch face.

We coasted into a gas station literally on fumes, and on the heels of me finding a good divorce attorney. With barely one eye open, I could see my husband standing next to the car, filling the tank and holding the debit card. Thoughts filled my mind: should I just drive off, but first, how can I get the debit card back? He was back in the car before I could consider option number two. I had been awake now for over 24 hours. Dazed and exhausted, we headed to the nearby hotel that accepted our four-legged Dixie girl. We were checking in when other guests were checking out. It had to have been around 6:00 a.m., and I think all three of us were exhausted. A quick few hours of sleep was all I needed as daylight was already upon us. Could this be a better day than the day before? I sure hoped so. I was too eager to drive and cautioned my passenger that I would take it from here. I also addressed my other passenger, Dixie, and said, "Momma's got this!" With fresh eyes, I could see the breadcrumbs, and I followed that trail leading us back home. We traveled hundreds and hundreds of miles each day, and because I was the passenger on the way out, landmarks became more noticeable, and I knew exactly where I was and the distance I needed to go before our next hotel stay. But within hours of being on the road, ADT sent me a notification that an entry had been made to the house. I called the listing agent, and she said she brought the Riverside buyer back through. She mentioned the buyer would like to purchase all the furniture purchased by the first buyer, so the first buyer would not have to rent a trailer and go back into the house to pick the items up.

And, of course, the new buyer only wants to pay half the original amount to the owner of the furniture. An immediate "No" rolled off my tongue. Stern, decisive, and steaming from what the agent just asked, I felt as though I was driving a steamroller at this point and was ready to roll over any other obstacle in my way. My passenger commented on my speed, my tailgating, and my cold shoulder. I didn't notice any of it. Back to Colorado for a night, then Iowa, and finally to Wisconsin. When I saw the "Welcome to Wisconsin" sign, he commented on my smile, and that made me smile even wider. For at that very moment, I left the bumper ahead of me, moved over into the left lane, and dropped my foot on the accelerator. The result of this was even more gratifying, for my car had California plates, and for the first and last time, I could drive like those assholes did to me in California and grin all the way. The speed limit in California wasn't directed at what speed to obtain and maintain, it was more like how much faster could we go? The car that I was once following decided to do the same and sped up to greet us on the right and gave my spouse the middle finger. Honestly, I think that was the most memorable part of the trip home, and it too made me smile. Blowing through Madison and onward to the lake house was triumphant. I was elated to be back, and it was Mother's Day on top of it.

Dixie had a new state and a lake house to explore. Green grass, milder temperatures, and a lake to plunge into. It was a new beginning but with familiarity. We were only 11 miles from where we departed the state, and now were undeniably home. When I unpacked the Suburban and carried in all the items, I inevitably carried in all the woes and lingering arguments, which included enormous disappointments. And of course, our house was left in the hands of our listing agent, with whom I lost trust in.

You can leave the state and troubles, but if you are thinking mileage will separate you from the heartache, you are sadly wrong. As I unpacked our belongings, I unpacked all the negativity that surrounded me in California. The stack of papers equating to two years of my life caught my eye every time I walked by the table, which held my efforts and not my outcome. I was merely going through the motions of being back and thinking that I should be happy when it didn't change a thing, because I didn't change a thing. Having lost faith in our listing agent, my husband geared up for flying back to California closer to the closing date so he could oversee the furniture pickup by the first party whose offer on our house fell through. But clearly at this point, I must admit, I believed they never intended to buy the house, and the $7,000 worth of furniture was just a way of keeping a pulse on our activity. Meaning, did we in fact move? Obviously getting into the house one more time would result in their answer. Nothing was left in the home except for what they purchased.

And by now, the movers who transported our household items back to Wisconsin had dropped off our possessions at a nearby storage facility. That too was a painful moment. Even though I was back, I was displaced. Life in storage again equated to life on hold. We first unloaded at the lake house rental, but because of the season, we only had a couple of weeks before we had to move to a short-term apartment rental. After the apartment rental, it was back to the lake house rental, and then hopefully to a final home. If this sounds appealing to anyone, please raise your hand (not just your middle finger).

I hope this story hasn't been as confusing for you to read as it was for me to live. But buckle up, there's more. The final closing of our home didn't release any funds to our account. And the response when calling the listing agent was, "Well, Ally, you have sold homes before, and you know the money doesn't transfer the same day." Well, folks, there you have it. Agents do not know everything and are as human as humanly possible, though some act like gods. Wow, I thought. I sold one home, and it was for sale by owner. Yes, the funds transferred the same day, and yes, the keys were handed over the same day. I truly believe this whole ordeal was the spark that led me to my new career in real estate.

That spark also ignited an argument between my husband and me, so I, in turn, took my frustration to the firepit outside. That evening, instead of using kindling and logs to start a fire, I lit a match to the 10-inch-thick stack of paperwork that had been weighing me down. The fiery glow emulated how I felt inside my heart, and as the red cinders glowed and the ashes gathered, I had the option of staying at the bottom of the firepit or gather up the faith to believe there would be a better tomorrow. And tomorrow was already going to be a challenge; I was heading to see the apartment into which we were moving. Our brief stay at the lake house would soon be ending, and on to the rental.

At the apartment complex, I was greeted by the sales manager Rachel and was asked if I would like a tour of the facility. I declined. I was just there to see the apartment. I didn't see this as an opportunity to start over and sadly admitted to myself that I was prideful. The sin of pride prevailed, and it stole my happiness. My unrealistic expectations laid me flat on my back. And the combination of my woes wreaked havoc on my body and mind. Anyone else would have taken it all in and enjoyed the ride. I preferred to be the pavement at this point and felt like the world was rolling over me.

Residing in an apartment caught me off guard. Perplexed and without an ounce of gratitude, I lamented over and over what felt like the demise of my life. I often reflected that I could be a chameleon when decorating for others, but I couldn't help myself adapt to my own environment.

My husband told me to bring the least amount I needed to survive, because in just four months, we would be moving back to the lake house rental. If that doesn't sound like a recipe for crazy, I don't know what does. By now, I was numb to it all.

Making the most out of the months at the apartment slowly became easier and easier, until the letter from the Bureau arrived. The letter stated there were insufficient findings in the case, and it was now closed. Even though the Bureau gave up, I didn't. I was not going to quit.

I became a nurse for my husband and younger son, who flew to Wisconsin to work for the summer. Both decided to have their tonsils out at the same time, and taking care of them was a nice diversion for me. I tried to enjoy the festivities happening right outside our patio door. With prime parking in front of our unit and tailgating right in our parking stall, the community was basically knocking at my door. Bands played weekly, special community events occurred monthly, and our apartment was within walking distance to bars and restaurants. Making the best of apartment living and, at the same time, trying to make the best of my life should have been easy, but I struggled.

I needed to conquer what seemed to conquer me. I was now determined to get my real estate license. I emailed the firm that I wanted to interview with, and immediately received a call from the sales director. The day of the interview, I vividly recall walking into the office and being greeted by a woman who stood up from behind her desk and acknowledged my presence. I also recall the gentleman who was to her right who was busy working away but took time to have a little chitchat as the woman walked away to let the sales director know I had arrived. The interview turned into a commitment, which turned into studying for the Wisconsin Real Estate exam.

By late August, I scheduled my exam, and the only individual who knew what I was up to was my younger son Cal. I thought he should be informed, for I was taking him back to California to get him ready for his junior year in college. When I heard the news, I couldn't have called Cal any faster, and the conversation was immediate – I passed. A huge sigh of relief on the other end of the line was the best accolade I could have received. Cal and I have been through a lot together, and this was a shared moment of joy. We were on target for having the best return trip to California possible. Of course, Cal been with his dad when I called, and as quickly as I had called my son, my husband called me. The secret Cal and I kept was revealed, and the surprise in my husband's voice was priceless, likewise was the surprise in Kevin's voice. Kevin, however, seems to know that the character of determination begins and ends with me. "Never give up." I think everyone was excited that I had turned the corner and was onto something much more rewarding than rehashing the prior experience! I believe the time I spent investigating the woes of California was growing on everyone's nerves. Keith especially was trying to put out the fire while I was still trying to pour gas on it. I just couldn't let it go. It was something that I didn't receive the right ending to, and it left me still searching.

Packing for a week back in California was a breeze this time around. A simple suitcase and carry-on were all I needed. Plans to decompress involved relaxation, meditation, and writing this book. The first leg of my trip was to focus exclusively on my son and get him ready for school. This was quite rewarding. It was just the two of us again, and I had the opportunity to model stamina and fortitude to accept challenges, do your best, and move on. Yes, I was slowly moving on, but truthfully, it didn't happen overnight. I needed a stronger power than the California Bureau of Real Estate to make it right, and honestly, I knew only God could help me. I am learning that I can change what I can control, adapt to what is adaptable, and compromise to give balance to things that are out of balance. And of course, make legal U-turns when necessary.

I wish I could tell you that things changed immediately, but they didn't. As soon as the plane landed in California, the old feelings came back. The white SUV at the airport intersection didn't necessarily comfort me. Nor did the experience I had when leaving. I left a day earlier than I had planned, and I was greeted at the airport with a man standing at the table with a newspaper, making eye contact with me as if acknowledging that yes, it was best that I was getting on a plane. I rehashed the entire list of events that had occurred while we lived in California. Is it a fact that one of the listing agent's best friends was a police officer? Yes. Could it have been a police officer who followed me into the HVAC showroom and asked, "What was that woman doing here?" Yes! Was the owner of the pickup truck outside the Home Depot and Mexican grocery shop the same person? Yes! Was that same man also the one staring at me at the airport? Yes! Did the listing agent also sell a home to the woman following me and the man at the Home Depot? Quite probably. Thanks to Google Maps, both vehicles are shown parked in the driveway of the home the agent sold. Could the attorney who stepped in to hear my story have been an attorney who also worked for the listing agent, or actual sellers? Quite possibly. What could have triggered such an interest in me? Was it concerning to "them" that someone from another state had discovered their story? Were drugs, money, money laundering, insurance and mortgage fraud a part of it? Did we receive more than what we bargained for? Theodore Roosevelt wrote, "Nobody cares how much you know, until they know how much you care." I personally cared too much to let it go! Letting go felt like quitting, and I didn't want to quit. Who changes title documents with that type of error? Perhaps it was beneficial to the borrower in efforts to pursue new investment properties. Three properties, to be exact, were acknowledged by the listing agent. Would you change your identity to protect yourself and move from firm to firm? The listing agent did. In two years, she changed firms three times. So many questions with so many more to ask. If our attorney told us to focus on the $90,000 kitchen remodel, then why didn't she have her assistant print a copy of the Zillow listing documenting this as evidence for our file? Why didn't the mediator cancel or postpone the mediation on his own accord of incorrect parties representing the seller? Why didn't my California friend come forward and say she was helping her nephew and missed insuring the built-in refrigerator with the home warranty? How ironic that the second home warranty company insured the house for the past five years. What a coincidence that the attorney had a fatal bike accident. And how ironic to see a white SUV and blonde-haired woman in the alley of the attorney's office.

Who was the man sitting in the Prius watching the restaurant? Who were the buyers that waited so long to pick up their furniture? If this were a movie, the plot and the characters were out in true Hollywood fashion. And if this were a TV series, perhaps it would be like *The Masked Singer*, only called *The Masked Real Estate Transaction*. But at the end, no one took off their mask.

But if credit could go to the character who missed his chance at the leading role and could have saved the day, it would go to the "nephew." The "if-I-knew" agent. If he only knew what he was supposed to know or, conceivably, if he had discovered it after the initial "What???" moment, this story and transaction wouldn't have been such a mystery to live or write. But I think he rang the commission bell before he began the mission.

The most recognizable character in this book, the one who was clearly identified to have lived in the house and would have known more than the walls if they could talk, was the dead black fly on the cooktop. I'm sure he was all the buzz until his life was snuffed out. But this cannot be the ending.

CHAPTER 29

The Art of Finding JOY

After my son Cal was settled in at his frat house, I headed to the desert to dry out my remaining emotions. The drive was intentional, and the winding road purposeful as well as soulful. Not knowing what was ahead of me as I drove through the mountains, I traveled carefully and ever so mindfully. Would I be tempted to spend my remaining days in California, starting the whole investigative process over again? Grace brought me through this experience, and I prayed that it would carry me through the rest of this week. God intentionally placed people in front of me and took others away.

I spent the time in the desert working out and clearing out my negative thoughts. According to my older son Kevin, I was "pounding sand." Push-ups, strength training, and bodybuilding encompassed my days. Writing this book took my thoughts that sometimes held me captive, to keystrokes on my laptop that set me free. I often slept in, which was a first for me, and sleep deprivation became obsolete. I listened to podcasts in the morning for positive reinforcement and relaxed in the evening with messages from our pastor, Rick Warren, in Lake Forest. During that week, I was also pleasantly surprised with a text message from Keith. Deliberate and impactful, it spoke to me directly, and I applaud my husband and Pastor Joyce Meyers for its place on my phone. "When you spend time with God, everyone knows. You become calmer, you are easier to get along with, you do not lose control of your emotions as quickly. Your patience increases, wisdom is manifested through you, and your heart soon understands what God likes and what offends Him. As with any friend, the more time you spend with God, the more you become like Him. Spend time with God today. Make it a priority. Your life depends on it because He is your vital necessity in life to prepare for the next."

Chapter 29 may be the chapter that each reader writes for themselves. The ending for some might just be the beginning for others. I was slow to understand defeat but wise to gravitate towards those who could help me and surpassed those who just got in my way. I struggled in California and still fall down the rabbit hole at times trying to understand it all. I know my character shined one day when I least expected it to, and it was grace that saved me that day. It was when we were living in California, in the middle of this real estate battle. I had driven about 10 minutes to a nearby city to go to a shop I frequented. When I drove into the parking lot, I could see the heat radiating from the black asphalt, the mirage of water. Then something more appeared. I saw the listing agent walking to her car with her three children. I knew my vehicle was bigger than hers, and I could have parked her in long enough to approach her to ask her all my questions, but I didn't. She was with her children, and God's grace told me to keep moving forward. So, I did.

I often find myself waiting on a letter from my California friend. I truly believe she is spiritual in nature, and I am hopeful that one day she too will be prompted to move forward and send me a note. Sometimes connections that are made are not worth losing, if you believe you can still achieve peace. I am a believer!

Looking back, it's interesting to me that in 2014, I didn't acknowledge what would be changing in my life. Yet, in 2015, I changed everything that was constant. I changed states, homes, my profession, family, and status to empty-nester. And yes, at 50, my apron strings were first cut from my mom and dad. Being 2,000 miles away was extremely difficult. In 2017, when we moved back to Wisconsin, my life changed again. This time, I felt that all of me didn't make the return trip. I found myself feeling as though I left something behind, beyond the investigation, yet I couldn't quite grasp what that was.

Getting my life back became my focus, and I relied on myself, my old creative self, and Eleanor Roosevelt, for she once said, "Great minds discuss ideas; average minds discuss events; and small minds discuss people." It took me two years of physically being back in Wisconsin to come up with an idea for how to regain my spirit. In March of 2019, my husband and I traveled back to California for a health and fitness expo in San Diego, and as he worked that week, I too continued to work on my new idea, and with the assistance of Green Scooters, sightseeing around the city made my idea more probable. It wasn't until May that it all unfolded. My husband and I returned once again to California for a family event, and as we celebrated, we appreciated how each of us had grown and conquered what we set out to achieve. However, for myself, I still had that lingering idea and it nudged me forward. By that following Monday, we were making our way back into San Diego to drop off our older son Kevin at the airport. Departure for one left me with the arrival of my idea to naturally unfold. I asked Keith if we could take a six-minute detour into the city, and he said, "Sure, are we sightseeing?" "No," I responded. "I am picking up something I left behind." I rolled down my window thinking I could read the addresses of the buildings more readily, however, that's when the cool air from the Pacific Ocean hit me along with the arrival of the cold brick building with small address, identifying we had met our destination.

It wasn't the discovery I was expecting. What I thought was supposed to be a place of helpful assistance resulted in the icy look of a morgue. I stared at the front doors made of glass and could see my reflection glaring back, waiting for my next move. I didn't share my motives, nor did I extend an invitation for Keith to join me. I hopped out and said, "Stay here, I will be right back." I meant it literally as well as figuratively.

I pulled on the right door handle, and it opened. I stepped inside and was immediately approached by a guard. As I explained why I was there, he pointed to the steel door to my left, which read "Suite 1063: Bureau of Real Estate." I believed this was the door that separated me from my happiness. The guard asked me to sign in, and I did. I proceeded to the steel door, and it opened. Walking down a small hall, I proceeded to a glass window and was soon approached by a woman asking if she could help me. I asked if Tami, the investigator who was working on my case, was in. The woman told me she was and would be out in a minute or two to speak with me. Amazing, I thought, even before she approached the glass window, which resembled a ticket station window, I would be able to have a conversation whether she wanted to hear it or not. Tami soon came forward; her face seemed to have aged, her hair cut shorter than before, and she sported an earphone that made me feel that she felt more important than she was. From there, I was able to re-introduce myself and reminded her of the investigation, the visit she made to our house, and the requests she made to me to investigate. I showed her a photo of the mother-daughter duo that she had asked me to produce: the listing agent and the blonde-haired woman. But from there, I put the photo down and proceeded with the true meaning of the visit. Regardless of how the investigation concluded, I told her what ended so poorly for me became my motivation to help others. I became a licensed real estate agent in the state of Wisconsin. My success as an agent comes from my clients' happiness. And for me, personally, it's all about the relationships. If you can't be trusted in establishing a relationship, how can you be entrusted with one of the biggest investments one could possibly make? Her response was her nature; she was silent. My morgue reference suits her well. She may not have heard a word I said, but I did. It resonated with me. The last door of this investigation closed when I chose to close it.

I returned to the rental car. As soon as my husband saw me, relief washed over his face. As we drove off, I explained why I had made that stop. But more importantly, I shared the experience I will never forget. I reconnected with the person, not an image or reflection in the glass doors. I took the initiative and entrusted myself with myself. "To thine own self be true," says Polonius in Hamlet, and Ally in Wisconsin.

I have reflected on the time spent lamenting over this event in my life, and I must admit, "If you could kick the person in the pants responsible for most of your trouble, you wouldn't sit for a month." Thank you again, Theodore Roosevelt, for the result of my misfortune consumed me and I let it. The not sitting for a month then allowed me to stand up, so I could see my future, my potential, and greatness on the horizon.

I have the opportunity today to share my passion for real estate with my dad, sister, and niece, along with the two aunts and my great-grandfather. Our passion for real estate, I believe, is derived from our passion for helping others.

Truth be told, my story has come full circle. The agent who came to my Pewaukee house is now my assistant sales director. And the assistant sales director prior to her appointment to sales director was, and still is, my real estate coach (and life coach, unbeknownst to her). And as I continue moving forward with a greater understanding of real estate, I have a greater understanding of me and the gifts God outfitted me with. My purpose in life has become far more meaningful and evolves around storing up treasures in Heaven. When you find God, you will find yourself. Your inner strength will lead you on, and your outward direction will guide you home.

It only gets better with time. Back in Wisconsin, I had more time to spend with my parents. I have a beautiful life. You are most like your Creator when you are creating, and when I implore that, I am happy.

I can't say I put down the magnifying glass completely, nor

can I say I had any other unexplainable happenings relating to our California experience. Most recently (August 2019), I noticed that Zillow referenced our old house in Norco as having a "Zub-Zero" refrigerator. Seeing how this was misspelled, I assumed this information had come from the previous "tenant." Little does she know, Sub-Zero is spelled with an "S" and the company is based out of Madison, WI. Remember, I was a decorator prior to my move. Also, as a rule in Wisconsin, and Illinois for that matter, car rental facilities very rarely have vehicles with heavily tinted windows. So, imagine my surprise when I found myself following a Corvette from Illinois down our dead-end road … I parked my vehicle in my neighbor's drive and walked towards the car. As I approached the driver's side window, I saw a woman in sunglasses with blonde hair. It made the hair on my arms stand up once again. Did the passenger roll down her window to say she was lost or was looking for a home in particular? "No, she did not!" Perhaps it isn't a closed case after all …

To say our Wisconsin home purchase was any easier would be saying it was uneventful, and it truly wasn't. But what has become even more interesting to me are the challenging obstacles that we either hurdle over or glide by. We fall flat on our face, or end up landing on our backs. It's recognizing that the smallest obstacle can debilitate us, and it's our mindset that keeps us down or picks us up.

I am "UP" for my next big adventure!

My next book captures some of the encounters that may land us on our backs; but with the ability to look up, we can get up! Look for *I Slipped on a Snowflake* (funny and positive, motivating, and inspirational) coming soon!

A must-read if you are human and have something that resembles a heart!

Warmest Regards,

Allison J. Diedrick

AFTERWORD

Today, as I sit at an old wooden table reclaimed as my desk, which my dad and I picked up at a resale store, I look at what is truly real. Beyond my laptop, small lamp, my grandfather's typewriter, and the chair with the rush seat, straight back, and armrests my sweet, dear friend gave me, I feel the real season of opportunity to move forward is upon me. Pausing on that last word, *forward*, with a little smile, I lift my eyes off my keyboard and notice that the wind has picked up. The tree that stands directly in front of my window is waving its branches and brushing them up against the side of the house. With my belief that there is a greater power, I believe the branches are nudging me forward to complete this season so I can move forward with my life and conquer what has been holding me back. Chapter 29 needed to be completed.

MEET ALLY

I was born in Illinois to parents God chose for me, and my world came alive as I did. Life labeled me a middle child, and it was much later in life that I labeled myself fortunate because of it. My siblings are my dearest friends, and we are intertwined beyond our DNA.

In my marriage of 28 years and counting, I am fortunate enough to say we are not growing old but wise. My children may have left the nest, but I no longer see it as empty. Our sons each have an empowered woman by their side, adding energy and new dynamics to our family.

Dixie, our rescue, rescued me. She is an amazing puppy dog. And if I were to write full-time, it would be because of her and her companionship.

God did not spell out how to become an author, but he gifted me the ability to tell my story. He did not say, "Now you are realtor," but he showed me the way and gave me the tenacity to become one, and hopefully a great one. And, he did not say, "You need to trade in your old self," he said, "You are growing into yourself." I feel this in my soul, and it has become a remarkable way of living. From yesterday to today, and if given a tomorrow, I see this all as a blessing, a gift, and an opportunity for greatness!

I have a BS degree from UW–Stout in Hotel Restaurant Management, secured a Field Marketing position earlier on with the Marcus Corporation, and found a personal interest of decorating, which turned into referral-based business and a brick-and-mortar store. I traveled out of my comfort zone to follow my husband to California, and when we moved back, I realized I could not find my own happiness without helping others find theirs.

My life has circled back exactly where I thought it ended and has provided me with a new beginning. As a realtor, I listed and sold my Pewaukee house for a second time. What an incredible opportunity. Where relationships are cultivated, the results are endless.

If you read my story, I believe your heart will skip a beat, and within that fraction of time, you will remember this story forever, but not as I wrote it, but somehow as you lived it.

Through your own eyes and personal experiences. As for myself, I had to write this book, for I believe we all need a Chapter 29 to move us forward in a way, to begin again.

Renewed in Faith.

Ally

Interface with the author, ask questions, engage in conversation.

Go to "Creative Agent - Ally Diedrick" on Facebook